The Best-Kept Secret

The Best-Kept Secret

WOMEN, CORPORATE LOBBYISTS, POLICY, AND POWER IN THE UNITED STATES

DENISE BENOIT

RUTGERS UNIVERSITY PRESS
New Brunswick, New Jersey, and London

μ—

LIBRARY OF CONGRESS CATALOGING-IN-PUBLICATION DATA

Benoit, Denise, 1955–
  The best-kept secret : women corporate lobbyists, policy, and power
in the United States / Denise Benoit.
    p. cm.
  Includes bibliographical references and index.
  ISBN-13: 978-0-8135-4065-8 (hardcover : alk. paper)
  ISBN-13: 978-0-8135-4066-5 (pbk. : alk. paper)
  1. Businesswomen—United States.   2. Corporations—United States—
Political activity.   3. Lobbying—United States.   I. Title.
  HD6095.B46 2007
  328.73'078082—dc22   2006031258

A British Cataloging-in-Publication record for this book is available
                      from the British Library

Visit out Web site: http://rutgerspress.rutgers.edu

Manufactured in the United States of America

To Luke Benoit Scott,
Who makes the world a better place

Contents

ACKNOWLEDGMENTS

FIRST AND FOREMOST, I am grateful to all of the men and women who participated in this project over the last decade. This book would not have been possible without their generosity and co-operation. I am especially thankful to the women government relations officials and staffers who took me to lunch, made me comfortable in their offices, and invited me to be part of their activities and events. They are, without a doubt, among the most highly educated, intelligent and articulate people I have ever met. Although it is the case that, as public relations specialists, these women are adept at interaction work, they seemed to be genuinely helpful, open, and candid. It is important to note that the analysis presented in this book is in no way meant to deni-grate or attack these women as individuals. They have worked extremely hard and made great strides to achieve well-paid and well-respected positions. They have taken corporate women from serving coffee to being substantially involved in the policy-making process on the national and state levels. And they have paved the way for future generations of women to enter posi-tions that were once well beyond their reach. This book does not criticize particular individuals (and, in any case, does not identify any of them by name because I promised them confidentiality), but rather critically examines larger systems and structures of power in the United States.

Although I take full responsibility for the materials pre-sented in this book, I am grateful to my esteemed colleagues who provided assistance at various stages of the project. Nancy

Folbre, Naomi Gerstel, and Jerry Himmelstein provided an important critique of my work at the earliest stages. I am most thankful to Dan Clawson, who never lets me down in his willingness and ability to provide detailed and constructive comments and suggestions on my work in addition to useful professional advice. I am very grateful for his generous support. Others who have been instrumental in my career development and who have given their valuable time and energy to provide feedback and support on this project are my highly esteemed colleagues Bill Domhoff and Pat Martin. Their work (Bill's on the power elite and Pat's on gendered organizations) shaped my thinking significantly during the writing of this book. I also thank David Cay Johnston for his helpful comments on chapter 3. His award-winning work on tax policy inspired me to write the chapter. I thank Kristi Long, former Rutgers University Press editor, for her interest in my work. I am extremely grateful to Adi Hovav, my current editor at Rutgers, whose excellent insights and creative suggestions along the way helped make this a stronger book. I also thank Adi for making the process as smooth as possible. Thanks also to Marilyn Campbell, director of the prepress department at Rutgers, Beth Kressel, assistant editor, and Nicholas Taylor, copyeditor, for their crucial attention to details. I am also very thankful for the useful suggestions and comments provided by the anonymous reviewers. I greatly appreciate their time and effort.

SUNY Geneseo is a top-rated liberal arts college that attracts high-caliber undergraduate students. Not only is Geneseo a great place to teach, it is an institution that also supports faculty research in a variety of ways. Throughout my tenure at Geneseo, I have received several grants to compensate students for their work as research assistants on this project. I am grateful to Kate Collins, Kate Phillips, Susan Drexel, Erin Quackenbush, and Courtney Volturno, who were enormously helpful in developing questions, reading through transcriptions and field notes, contributing to the theoretical framework, and editing materials. I also thank Kelly Boeing, Christi Papagakis, and April Hirsh for their editorial work on parts of the manuscript. Last but not least, Joyce Peter, our department secretary, saved my life more than once with her keen eye for typos and help with formatting and preparing the manuscript. I am very grateful for her help.

Several grants supported the research for this book. National Science Foundation Grant SES-9001440 provided funding at the initial stages of the project. I also received support from the Nuala McGann Drescher Grant and Leave Program, funded jointly by the United University Professions and SUNY Geneseo. Generous support was also provided by SUNY Geneseo in the form of several Geneseo Foundation Incentive and Travel Grants for which I am very grateful. None of the organizations that provided support is responsible for, or endorses, the views expressed in this book.

Lastly, I would not have been able to complete this book without the generous help of friends and family. Thanks to my "Starbucks friends" for providing encouragement, great discussion, and an occasional much-needed coffee break throughout the course of writing this book. I am also very thankful for the endless support of my family: Glenn Scott and Luke Benoit Scott; Cecile Benoit; Jeff, Theresa, Cassandra, and Amanda Benoit. As an equal partner in housework and childcare, and as a constant source of support in many other ways, Glenn deserves a huge amount of credit for the completion of this work. I am very grateful to him. Luke never failed to bring a smile to my face even during the most difficult parts of the process. Luke also contributed enormously to the successful completion of the manuscript with his practical advice and computer expertise at several critical points. And I cannot forget Hannah, Andy, and Zoe, who warmed my feet while I plucked away at the computer.

The Best-Kept Secret

CHAPTER 1

Introduction

POWER IS ONE of the most complex and dif-
ficult concepts in the social and political sciences, partly because
there are so many competing definitions, and partly because
many key decisions are made behind closed doors. At the same
time, the analysis of power is critical to our understanding of
how the world works. To examine the processes and structures
of power in the United States and around the world is to develop a better understanding of the forces that shape our organizations, institutions, relationships, and, as a consequence, our
own opportunities and experiences. Any hope for social change
rests on our attention to power.

Most scholarly and journalistic analyses of political-economic power in the United States focus on men at the top—
corporate heads, politicians, hired guns—those who have the
final say in making policy decisions or have direct authority
or influence over those who do so or both. This book takes
the analysis of power in the United States one step down and
one step further by looking at a group that has received very
little attention in the media and scholarly literature—the ever-
growing cadre of in-house corporate-government relations officials who work largely behind the scenes lobbying for corporate interests in the political realm, and, in particular, women
lobbyists, whose numbers over the last few decades have increased dramatically relative to men but fall even further below
the radar screen. What is the significance of this new face of

corporate lobbying for creating and reproducing systems and structures of power? Does gender have anything to do with it? Who benefits and who loses as a result? Academics and the media have largely ignored these questions, and yet they are critical to our understanding of equality and democracy in the United States.

CORPORATE POWER

In *Who Rules America*, G. William Domhoff (2002, 10–13) lists three indicators of who holds power in our society: 1) Who benefits? 2) Who governs? and 3) Who wins? With regard to who benefits, although those with the most income and wealth are not necessarily the most powerful, "income and the possession of great wealth are visible signs that a class has power in relation to other classes." Power can also be inferred by looking at which group, or class, occupies important decision-making positions in a particular society. As Domhoff notes, the "who governs" indicator is not perfect because official positions of power may not in fact hold much power, and because groups or classes may exhibit and maintain power from behind the scenes. The third indicator, "who wins," is the one employed most by social scientists and the one I use in this book. This indicator is most important in measuring power for the same reason it is problematic. Important decisions are made and policy set in ways that are hard to see because the process is by and large convoluted, confusing, takes place away from public view, and because non-decisions are often more advantageous to certain groups than decisions. However, when social scientists manage to untie the knots, put the puzzle pieces together, and when a few even manage to get behind the scenes, use of this indicator clearly and convincingly points us to corporations as holding enormous and unequal power in the United States. The corporate community "controls the public agenda and then wins on most issues that appear on it" (or prevents them from appearing at all) through several different, but over-lapping, processes (Domhoff 2002, 12):

1. The special-interest process
2. The policy-planning process
3. The candidate-selection process
4. The opinion-shaping process

This book concentrates on the first process through which corporations, individually and as a whole, work to access and influence those who make public policy.

Corporate lobbyists, lawyers, and various other corporate-government relations officials are central to the special interest process through which corporations exert and maintain enormous influence in the political realm. Bartlett and Steele (1998, 2) define corporate welfare as "a game in which governments large and small subsidize corporations large and small, at the expense of another state and town and almost always at the expense of individual and other corporate taxpayers . . . The Federal Government [is] America's biggest sugar daddy, dispensing a range of giveaways from tax abatements to price support for sugar itself." At a time when welfare for individuals and families has been cut at the national level, Congress continues to enact legislation that provides large subsidies to business. Corporate lobbyists and other government relations personnel are key to the growth of corporate welfare. Often in behind-the-scene settings, such as secluded resorts and spas, Washington lobbyists get together with legislators, legislative aides, and Internal Revenue Service (IRS) and Treasury officials, to "exchange ideas" about public policy. On August 7, 2002, thousands of legislators and corporate lobbyists gathered in Orlando, Florida, to play golf and listen to speeches. They also drafted bills, like the one that would require state governments to deregulate electric utilities, repeal minimum-wage laws, limit class-action lawsuits against companies, privatize public pensions, and compensate property owners for environmental regulations that restrict land use (Olsson 2002).

THE FACE OF LOBBYING

In the last few decades we have seen an explosion of both journalistic reports and scholarly works that critically examine the relationship between special interests, public policy, and power. However, it wasn't until the notorious Jack Abramoff, one of the most powerful hired guns in Washington, entered the spotlight that the dubious practices of lobbyists were in full public view. A recent article in the *Economist* (2006) states that the number of registered Washington lobbyists has doubled in the last five years, to over 35,000. Yet it is the media's relatively recent focus on high-profile cases like the Abramoff scandal that has focused attention on the widespread use of money, trips, and networking by lobbyists to obtain favors from government officials. We couldn't get away from the Abramoff story. It headlined every newspaper and TV news show for months. If we didn't know Jack before the scandal, we certainly did in the aftermath.

Among the many indictments against Abramoff was the charge that he and his buddy Michael Scanlon bilked a half-dozen Indian tribes out of millions of dollars by taking their money and funneling it through a series of nonprofit organizations and advocacy groups (including the Americans for Tax Reform, headed by Abramoff's longtime crony Grover Norquist) to compensate themselves and buy influence—sometimes resulting in legislation that opposed the tribes' interests (Galloway 2006a, E3). Casino-owning Indian tribes were contributing more that $5 million to influence pro-gambling legislation; some of which, after being funneled through a series of nonprofit organizations in order to "obscure the source of the funds," went to Ralph Reed, former head of the Christian Coalition, to mobilize Christian groups to advocate for anti-gambling legislation (Galloway 2006b, E1). Abramoff and Scanlon also funneled

$50,000 from two Indian tribes through the National Center for Public Policy Research to pay for a luxury $120,000 golf trip to St. Andrews, Scotland (Schmidt 2004; Smith 2005, 4; 2006, A9). Included on the trip, besides Abramoff and Scanlon, were Reed; David Safavian, former White House budget official who worked with Abramoff prior to his government post; Tom DeLay, then Senate majority leader and Scanlon's former boss; Tony Rudy, former deputy chief of staff to DeLay; and Representative Ney (R-Ohio), often called the "Mayor of Capitol Hill" because of his influential role (Borger 2005).

Abramoff was, without a doubt, the king of connections in Washington. His close allies ranged from lifelong friends including Norquist, Scanlon, and Reed, to key people in business, government, and the media. There is, for example, Doug Bandow, the Copley News Service syndicated columnist who wrote as many as twenty-four op-eds favorable to Abramoff's clients (Birnbaum 2005). And then there is Abramoff's friend Timothy Flanigan, vice president and chief council at Tyco International Ltd. (and former White House deputy counsel). Tyco paid $1.7 million to Abramoff's law firm between 2003 and 2004 in an "effort to block the Corporate Patriot Enforcement Act" and similar bills designed to penalize American firms that incorporated outside the United States (mostly to avoid taxes.). The bill was blocked. Tyco moved corporate headquarters to Bermuda in 1997 (Roche 2005, A10).

Along with Jack Abramoff and his fellow lobbyists, high-powered men in all areas of business and government have begun to receive a great deal of public attention and criticism in recent years. From corporate executives like Enron's Kenneth Lay and Jeffrey Skilling, to Dick Cheney and George Bush, nearly every recent scandal has focused on men at the top. When women are taken into account, it is usually not as central or influential players but as wives, daughters, and fiancées on the periphery. Judy Doolittle, wife of Representative John Doolittle; Lee

Rudy, wife of Tony Rudy; Christine DeLay, wife of Tom DeLay; Wendy Buckman, wife of lobbyist Edwin Buckman; and Pamela Abramoff, Jack's wife, are referred to as the "Wives Club" by FBI agents (Shenon 2006, A26). For their part in the Abramoff case, the media described them as "caught up in the scandal" or "orbiting Abramoff's world" (Shenon 2006, A26; Schmidt and Grimaldi 2005, A1). Even when women are clearly central to the policy-making process, they are largely viewed as an appendage. Take the case of thirty-three-year-old Suzie Stevens Matthews, whose father, Charlie Stevens, is an influential lobbyist on Capitol Hill. Suzie was "pivotal in winning one of the most heavily lobbied bills from last session—one, in fact, that was so important to the liquor industry that there were as many as twenty lobbyists working it in hallways at one time." Yet in the newspaper clippings, when she got mentioned, it was followed with "daughter of Charlie Stevens" (Bodfield 2002).

The relatively recent flurry of lobbying scandals reflect and fuel the commonly held perception of political influence, and power more generally, as related to men and masculinity. When we hear the term "lobbyist," what comes to mind for most people is a group of men who linger in the halls of Congress, wine and dine legislators, and sometimes engage in dubious practices in order to gain access and influence. Although women are now a common sight on the lobbying scene in Washington, D.C., and elsewhere in the country (half of all lobbyists at the state level are women), we still tend to think of an old-boy's network of corporate and government representatives who meet at places like the Bohemian Grove where they pee on trees and share "Bulls Balls" lunches (Domhoff 1974).

It is true that, until roughly thirty years ago, women's lobbying activity was mostly restricted to "women's issues," when "it was uncommon to see a woman standing at the third floor rotunda railing jawboning a lawmaker" (Nickel 2004). That is no longer the case. Women increasingly occupy influential positions as Washington lobbyists and political consultants and are now found lobbying both federal and state legislatures on a broad range of policy issues. And yet popular notions of this work remain closely tied to how we conceptualize and define men's and women's interests: men's interests as related to the public sphere, women's the private. When reporters and political pundits do pay attention to women's lobbying activity, it is typically restricted to their work in areas such as healthcare, education, family planning, or, more generally, "women's rights." As Linda Tarplin, a top Washington health care lobbyist and part of an all-women health care lobbying company, says, "In the healthcare world, there are a lot of strong women lobbyists" (Birnbaum 2006). Women also receive attention for their lobbying efforts on behalf of women's rights around the world. For example, news reports have highlighted women's efforts to ratify the Women's Rights Treaty, which requires signatory countries to "ensure that all women and girls have access to adequate health care facilities, including information, counseling, and services in family planning" (Archibald 2002). Women's lobbying groups also receive attention for their efforts on behalf of HIV victims around the world. The media consistently highlights lobbying efforts by both anti- and pro-abortion women's groups. For example, calls by women groups for the withdrawal of Harriet Miers from Supreme Court Justice consideration, mostly because of her stance on "women's issues," received a great deal of attention. Some were quoted as arguing that Miers looked like "Anthony Scalia in a skirt," others that her stance on abortion rights was too liberal (Hurt 2003; Hurt and Hallow 2005).

Likewise, social science research tends to focus on women's involvement in shaping policy related to women's interests in the private sphere, such as welfare and family policy (Folbre 2001; Misra 1998a, 1998b, 2002; Orloff 2001). Women's increased involvement in corporate lobbying, particularly in areas such as taxes and defense, has thus gone relatively unnoticed. Partly this is because these policy areas are not seen as related to women's interests. It is also because most of the attention to issues of policy and power tends to concentrate on those at the top of business and government, who are mostly men, rather than those who occupy second-tier positions, where women have entered in greater numbers.

CONCEPTUALIZING POWER

There is an overwhelming tendency among social scientists to focus on formal, coercive, and dominant forms of power. Dahl, Weber, and Mills are examples of theorists who adhere to this conception. Sociologists and political scientists who analyze corporations and governments tend to use structural definitions of power. Likewise, most researchers of organizations and occupations typically use a structural or formal approach when examining inequality and power; those at the top of the organizational hierarchy are most often characterized as powerful. Researchers who study gender stratification and inequality also tend to attribute power to those in structurally dominant positions—specifically white men.

Feminist theorists (Hartsock 1983, 1990; Pitkin 1972) argue that definitions of power as domination and control are rooted in male life experiences, and traditionally theorized by men. These theories fail to address the genderedness of power and its importance in structuring human relations. An alternative definition of power is one that stresses not only domination, but also "capacities, abilities, and strengths" (Hartsock 1990, 158). "Stressing power as energy or capacity," says Hartsock, "directs attention away from relations of domination" (1983, 22). Bookman and Morgen (1988, 19) further note that women's empowerment is visible in the "transformation of their views of themselves as women and in their capacity to understand and change the world they live in." This alternative view of power as "influence" or transformative, rooted in women's experiences, broadens our perspective and holds open the possibility for change (Scott 1996).

Influence, or transformative power, is evident in women's connections with other women at similar levels. Women corporate-government relations officials and legislative staffers may not have the final say, as do government officials and corporate heads, but, as shown in this book, they are nevertheless instrumental in influencing policy. Further, the connections they establish help to solidify women's common identity and serve as the basis for political consciousness and action, in much the same way women's networks and organizations during the Victorian Era provided the basis for solidarity, resistance, and empowerment. Thus, this book argues that women in society are placed in a somewhat compromised and conflicted position with regard to the increase in women's representation as lobbyists. On one hand, through their positions and relations, women lobbyists enhance corporate power and their own individual status. On the other hand, they act and interact in ways that reflect and reinforce persistent gender ideologies that serve to disadvantage and burden women as a group. Drawing from interview, participant-observation, survey, and secondary data collected over a ten-year period, this book is the first to provide a close look at the women who lobby in the interest of major corporations in the United States and examine the consequences of their activities and interactions for corporate power and for women as a whole.

THE RESEARCH

I became interested in women's entry into corporate lobbying, and the area of corporate-government affairs more generally, over a decade ago while working on *Money Talks: Corporate PACs and Political Influence* (Clawson et al. 1992). While conducting interviews with corporate PAC officials in

Washington for the book, I noticed that many of our interviewees were women. Although not the focus of the book, I suggested to my coauthors that we include interview questions related to women's entry into the profession. Those thirty-nine initial interviews provided the first glimpse of the world of women corporate-government relations officials and provided a basis for my research in this area.

I subsequently conducted my own set of twelve in-depth interviews with men and women lobbyists and PAC managers who work for top U.S. corporations in Washington. Although they do not like to call themselves "lobbyists," all of the corporate-government relations officials interviewed for this book network with those in government and seek to gain information and access in the legislative realm. Some are registered lobbyists. This first set of interviews also included eight men and women who head Washington lobbying and PR firms, as well as the heads of women's networking and policy organizations, including National Abortion Rights Action League (NARAL), National Organization of Women (NOW), and Women in Government Relations. All of the interviews were semi-structured, all were taped, and all interviewees were promised confidentiality. Interview questions centered mostly on the interviewees' career histories, what they do in their jobs, how they view their opportunities as shaped by their gender, the character and frequency of their relations with others in business and government, and the relationship between family and work. The interviews lasted anywhere from forty-five minutes to an hour and a half.

These interview data helped clarify important questions to include in a subsequent mail survey and provide a context within which to interpret the survey results. The mail survey was administered to men and women government relations officials at 231 corporations. After a series of follow-ups, both mail and phone, I managed to achieve a response rate of 70 percent. This response rate compares very favorably to other studies of corporate-government relations officials and corporate executives (Sabato 1984). Fifty-eight percent of the survey respondents are men, forty-two percent women. Most of the respondents held the titles of manager or director of government affairs, although they ranged from legislative assistant to vice president. All of the respondents interacted regularly with those in government; many were registered lobbyists. The survey questions included demographic variables such as gender, age, number of children, marital status, years in government relations work, title, career experience, educational background, and salary. It also contained questions concerning the structure and nature of the respondents' networking activity. To examine the *scope* of interactions, respondents were asked the number of corporate officials, legislative aides, and legislators with whom they interacted within a two-month period. To examine the *character* of their interactions, respondents were asked not only with whom they interacted, but also in what context. Did they meet for breakfast or lunch, have dinner together, see a play, go to a baseball game? Respondents were also asked roughly what percentages of these contacts were women.

Although the interview and survey data provided important knowledge and information concerning women's entry into lobbying, their jobs and career backgrounds, and the structure of women's work and family ties, they did little to advance an understanding of how corporate lobbyists go about influencing government, or the significance of women's entry into the field, their connections, and gender, for maintaining corporate power. A major shortcoming of the existing research is that it does not get inside places where connections between those in business and government are established and nurtured, and where decisions are made. Because academics typically do not have access to these places, most social research in this area relies on secondary data and inference. Thus, during the spring of 1999 I conducted participant-observation research at the annual retreat of the Tax

Alliance (pseudonym), located at a hotel and spa tucked away on a mountainside in the eastern part of the United States.

The Tax Alliance is composed of 125 women who represent business and government, specifically in the area of taxes. Members are lobbyists and other government relations officials who represent the political interests of many of the largest corporations and trade associations in the United States, as well as Washington lawyers and public affairs consultants whose firms represent major U.S. businesses. Tax Alliance members also include women who work as congressional aides and counsel to important tax-related policy committees and administrative departments within government (e.g., Committee on Ways and Means, U.S. Senate Finance Committee, U.S. Treasury).

Each spring, the Tax Alliance women come together in the relaxed and luxurious setting of a secluded resort and spa. In attendance during the spring of my research were five counsels and public liaisons to the U.S. Treasury; three high-level advisors to key governmental tax and finance committees (Ways and Means, House and Senate Finance); eight congressional staffers representing members who serve on important tax-writing committees; twenty government relations officials representing the top financial and industrial corporations in the United States; and nine representatives of chief business-related trade associations. The remainder of the participants were lawyers and consultants representing over thirty-six major U.S. companies.

Attendance at the retreat is normally restricted to members of the Tax Alliance and guests (family); it is highly unusual for academics, reporters, or other outsiders to be permitted entry. I was fortunate to be granted access by the organization's board through the support of a key person in the organization, a woman I met while conducting my initial interviews.

Upon arrival at the resort I was given an identification badge, a huge binder, and other various materials related to the meeting. I participated in all scheduled events, including the

formal sessions each morning and all formal luncheons and dinners. I participated in the bowling tournament, the "Sequins
Only" banquet, and the spa activities. I took advantage of every
possible opportunity to engage in informal dialogue with participants, joining women in the hospitality suite following the
formal sessions and after dinner, joining other participants for
breakfast, lunch, or afternoon tea, and during free time walking
about the grounds of the hotel and spa hoping to strike up an
impromptu chat.

During the year following the retreat I conducted twenty
in-depth, semi-structured interviews with corporate lobbyists
and congressional staff in Washington, D.C. Interviewees were
selected from among the women I met or spoke with at the retreat. I also included three male staffers. The interviews focused
mostly on clarification and interpretation of issues and questions
that arose from my participant-observation research. They lasted
anywhere from thirty minutes to an hour and a half; the average was one hour. Eighteen of the interviews were taped and
transcribed. Of the two that were not taped, one interview took
place in a cafeteria where the noise level dampened any hope
for a clear recording. The other interview took place at a ritzy
Georgetown restaurant frequented by high-level business and
government representatives, where a recorder would have been
obtrusive and potentially damaging to the rapport developed
between the researcher and subject. In order to honor my promise of strict confidentiality, neither individuals nor the organizations or government officials with which they are affiliated are
identified in this book; therefore, quotes omit any identifiers.

The book also draws from secondary data sources. I used
Washington Representatives and the *Legislative Staff Directory* to
obtain data with regard to the organization and composition
of corporate-government relations offices and legislative staffs. I
also draw from publicly available data provided by the Center for
Responsive Politics, the Citizens for Tax Justice, and the IRS.

OVERVIEW OF THE BOOK

In the last few decades, significant changes have occurred in the level and character of women's lobbying activity in the United States. Women are increasingly fighting for interests related to organizations in the public sphere, specifically corporations. Chapter 2 begins by placing women's corporate lobbying in social-historical context by examining changes in the nature of women's political action over time, and the political-economic structures and dominant ideologies that shaped these changes. We then shift to women on the contemporary lobbying scene in the United States. Where exactly do we see women lobbyists at the state and federal level today, and particularly in the area of corporate lobbying, where women have made the most advances? Few women have risen to the ranks of the hired guns in Washington, but women are making significant headway as lobbyists *within* corporations' government affairs operations. What positions do they occupy within the corporate hierarchy? In which policy areas do they concentrate?

Chapter 2 also provides a look at the work of corporate lobbyists. What are lobbyists? What do they do in their jobs on a daily basis? We examine the importance of connections in the work of corporate lobbyists and ask whether the character and scope of men's and women's networks differ. This chapter further discusses the significance of lobbying for the corporate bottom line and raises questions regarding women's empowerment through government affairs work and its significance for corporate-government relations and corporate power.

The significance of women lobbyists' recent entry into formerly male policy realms, such as taxes and social security, is further explored in chapter 3. Although taxes and social security are not typically seen as women's issues, women increasingly occupy positions as corporate lobbyists and as legislative aides who specialize in these policy areas. They are also forming women-only organizations and policy discussion groups where they can they keep abreast of what is happening in business and government with regard to these areas.

Although corporate welfare in the form of tax breaks and other concessions has flourished in the last few decades, welfare for women and families has been significantly cut. In fact, tax reform has consistently penalized women, particularly those who are married and work outside the home. Chapter 3 explores the significance of women's involvement in corporate lobbying in the areas of tax and social security policy for the interests of women as a whole. Although these issues are typically not seen as women's issues, corporate tax breaks have a huge effect on women and other groups in the United States. It is partly because of the false public-private sphere dichotomy that we lose sight of the effects of women's actions in the public sphere on women's conditions in the private sphere. In this chapter I examine how and why women's work as corporate lobbyists may be antithetical to women's interests as a whole.

Chapter 4 takes a look at the inner-workings of the Tax Alliance, a women-only Washington policy discussion group consisting of top corporate and trade association lobbyists and other government relations personnel, legislative staff, and counsel to key tax-writing committees in government. The Tax Alliance women come together each spring to enjoy gourmet meals, soak in the spa, play golf, hike, and discuss key policy issues. This chapter analyzes the significance of the women's activities and interactions at the retreat for the strength of business-government relations and the power of business in the United States. Further, it asks how and why the Tax Alliance women do and use[1] gender at the retreat. What are the consequences of doing and using gender for business-government relations? For women's opportunities and power? Do women see the character of their connections as different than those of men? How do their activities differ? Does soaking in the spa differ from engaging in competitive sports as a way to create and nurture business-government ties?

I argue that the tax family created and maintained at the retreat, nurtured through various activities and events, such as the "Sequins Only" banquet and the bowling tournament, helps ensure that corporate representatives have an ear in government in times of need. The nature of their career paths also helps in creating networks of obligation between women in government and corporate women. Further, through their actions and activities, the Tax Alliance women do and use gender at the retreat in ways that contribute to the strength of the business-government alliance and at the same time reinforce gender difference in ways that may be limiting to women.

No study of women in the workforce would be complete without an analysis of family relations. As with women's positions and relations in the workplace, women's family relations are more likely than men's to be viewed as bonds of love and affection, expressive rather than instrumental, hence not useful or empowering. Drawing from interviews and survey data, chapter 5 looks at the limitations and opportunities provided by the family ties of women who work as corporate lobbyists and legislative staffers.

Women lobbyists and legislative staff are differently positioned than their male colleagues vis-à-vis their homes and families. They spend more hours on childcare and housework than their male counterparts and consequently are more limited in the time they can spend on their work as lobbyists. Also, as wives and mothers, they report having to work harder in their jobs in order to be taken seriously. Betsy Mitchell, lobbyist and owner of a corporate consulting firm, admits that "it's tough to be a conscientious mom and a lobbyist" (Nickel 2000). But, as chapter 5 argues, women lobbyists also derive significant social and political capital through their relations with family members who work on the Hill.

The concluding chapter further analyzes the implications of changes in women's lobbying over time, and specifically women's movement into corporate lobbying. How and why does women's lobbying activity make a difference with regard to women's status and position within society? How does it make a difference in the nature of corporate-government relations and the strength of corporate power? *The Best-Kept Secret* argues that, because women's work and interactions as corporate public relations and government relations specialists are not typically viewed as "instrumental" compared to other managerial and professional positions, we tend to ignore the part women play in shaping policy in this area. This is a mistake. Through their involvement in a broad range of policy areas, and through their activities and interactions in and out of the workplace, women are a significant force in strengthening corporate-government relations and shaping public policy. Finally, social scientists are just beginning to understand the importance of knowing how and why "people mobilize around gender and sexuality, the rewards and costs of doing so," and, further, how the construction and use of gender is situation-specific (Martin 2001, 1993; Martin and Collinson 1999, 300). This book argues that women do and use gender in ways that make them enormously effective in their jobs as corporate lobbyists, at the same time reinforcing structures and ideologies that serve to oppress women.

If we are to fully understand the processes and structures of power in the United States, we need to shift our lenses to focus on women's role in shaping policy in all areas of society. To do this, we must begin by redefining women's issues to include those policy areas commonly thought of as related to the public sphere, and thus men and masculinity. This is particularly important at a time when women are rapidly entering positions where they lobby for interests commonly thought of as related to the public sphere. This book thus begins by asking how and why women have come to lobby for public-sphere interests, what they do in their jobs, and why it matters.

CHAPTER 2

From Private to
Public Interests

WOMEN'S ENTRANCE INTO
CORPORATE LOBBYING

WOMEN ARE RELATIVELY new to corporate lobbying but nevertheless have long been active agents in shaping political and economic structures and processes in the United States. Historically, as women became engaged in formal education, travel, and work outside the home, they began to develop an identity as women, and as such began to exert a unified voice in the public realm. Although women did not acquire the right to vote and hold office until 1920, they were actively involved in struggles for moral reform and protective labor legislation throughout the 1800s and early 1900s. By the latter decades of the twentieth century, the Women's Movement, along with increased participation in the paid labor force, had provided them with legitimacy and credibility in the political realm. Women began to mount vigorous, extensive, and often successful, lobbying campaigns for educational and workplace equality. Today, according to Nownes and Freeman (1998), over three-quarters of female lobbyists in Washington, D.C., work for groups that focus on family, children's, reproductive, or other women's interests. At the same time, the last few decades have witnessed the rapid movement of women into lobbying areas once considered the sole province of men, such as corporate lobbying and in policy areas such as taxes and social security. Although largely unnoticed by social and political scientists, women corporate lobbyists have become an increasingly significant force in the relationship between business and government in the United States.

From "Private" to "Public" Interests

As early as the seventeenth century, learned women attempted to rally support for the right of women to a formal education. These early "lobbyists" faced tremendous adversity. Any attempt by women to challenge prescribed gender roles, especially doing so in public, was seen as a serious threat to social stability. Physicians diagnosed such women as "sexually immoral," even "mad." Anna Maria van Schurman, who wrote a book advocating for women's formal education, was condemned for her audacity. The Duchess of Windsor, Margaret Cavendish, was persecuted for publishing her written work. Labeled "Mad Madge," she eventually retired to the countryside in quiet abandonment of her fight (Whitaker 2002).

During the 1700s and 1800s women were much more likely than men to be literate, even though they were much more politically restricted. Formal education for women was agreed on by the society at large (Cott 1977, 105). If women were to be competent mothers, that is to teach children about liberty and representation, moral ethics, and economic principles of prudence, frugality, and accountability, they had to be properly educated. By 1840, almost all women could read and write (Cott 1977, 16). White, middle-class, and wealthy women of English Protestant heritage, and single women in particular, spent a great deal of time reading and writing.

Education helped reinforce women's role and identity as wives and mothers, but also had the unintended consequence of leading women to look beyond their place in the domestic sphere, to see themselves as actors in the public realm. They attended academies for women "scholars," where they were taught needlework, foreign language, painting, music, and other subjects that prepared them for teaching. During the late 1700s and early 1800s, women often traveled to find jobs as teachers. They often ventured away from their families and communities to teach summer school. Women also worked as writers,[1] midwives, and trusted healers. In the mid–1800s, women formed maternal and moral reform societies where they gathered to read appropriate works, network with other women, and use their pious influence to have a political impact (Cott 1977).

Throughout the seventeenth and eighteenth centuries, women were active, if not in an auxiliary role, in the anti-slavery movement. They circulated petitions, organized women's groups, and raised money (Simon and Danziger 1991). By 1837, women had formed the Anti-Slavery Convention of American Women. Most of their activities involved petitioning, getting the word out, and rallying support for the cause. Although women's involvement in the anti-slavery movement eventually dissipated, it nonetheless provided a basis for later political action, and specifically women's involvement in lobbying activity. It taught them how to write, speak, and network. Middle- and upper-class women, in particular, were more likely to live in urban areas, where they had more access to politics and to connections with other women (Cott 1977, 14).

Women also gained social, political, and educational capital through the formation of maternal and moral reform associations during the mid–1800s and at the turn of the century (Cott 1977; Ryan 1979). More than 400 chapters of the American Female Moral Reform Society sprung up through New England and the mid-Atlantic states in the 1830s and 1840s (Ryan 1979, 67). These associations provided women with the opportunity to form reciprocal interpersonal relations and an identity as women with interests and issues apart from, but not necessarily inferior to, those of men. In some ways their political activities reflected a moral superiority among women who lobbied for policy that would restrain masculinity and bring about moral order; in other words, "sooth the savage beast" (Cott 1977, 167). As the moral caretakers of society, women joined to petition for an end to licentiousness. They took to the streets with their fight to curb the bad habits of men in particular, including drunkenness and solicitation of prostitution, so as to promote a morally straight foundation for the next generation. Through their common experiences and purpose, women formed an identity and "collective destiny" both as women and as public actors. Moreover, they formed a sisterhood, a female community that provided them with a resource outside the family (Cott 1977).

Likewise, the young women who worked in the early factories during the 1800s established a common identity and bond that provided a basis for political action. The first factories actively solicited the employment of women, mostly young and single, from surrounding areas. They were assumed to be a relatively docile work force willing to work for less pay than their male counterparts. But women struggled hard against the oppressive conditions in the factories and won concessions in the form of better conditions and higher wages. They earned significant respect through their work and actions. As Dublin (1994) observes, women worked along side each other in the factories and lived in close quarters in factory housing. Because of their homogeneity (white, Protestant, young, single), their living and working arrangements, and the pressure toward conformity that arose from these conditions, these women formed a gender consciousness and a solid bond that enabled them to struggle successfully against the companies.

Nevertheless, the rise of industrial capitalism, and corresponding dual spheres ideology and cult of true womanhood, that took firm hold in the United States limited women's utility and power by defining men's issues as those connected with the cold and rational public sphere, women's issues with private sphere and matters of the "heart." The dual spheres ideology essentially asserted that women's place is in the home, men's in the market. Women came to be seen as responsible for "implanting ideas and cultivating dispositions" in children (Cott 1977) and, more generally, improving and maintaining the moral character of family and community. Along with the development of this ideology came the cult of domesticity, the idea that the home is associated with love and affection, and that functions performed in the home should not be viewed as work but as acts of love (Cancian 1986; Cott 1977). Thus, women's work in the home came to be devalued relative to men's work in the market, which was seen as instrumental and productive.

These ideologies did not reflect the reality of all women's lives. African American women have worked outside the home historically, as slaves and servants in white people's homes, then as domestics. Poor women and immigrant women also worked outside the home to support their families. Many families simply could not afford the dual spheres ideology to be a reality in their lives. A significant proportion of all factory operatives in New England around the turn of the century were immigrants. Nevertheless, the dual spheres ideology and cult of domesticity affected the lives of all women and significantly shaped the extent and nature of their political activity. Women's interests came to be seen as those related to the private sphere of home and family, men's to the public sphere of work and the economy. More than this, early feminists agreed that the interests of men in business and government were "selfish and denigrating," compared to the altruistic interests of women in the private sphere (Cott 1977).

At the same time, early access to formal education, bonds established with other women, and (limited) experiences as public actors gave women the tools they needed for later participation in the policy realm and instilled in them a sense of women as part of the political process, as political actors, at the local and national levels. By 1869, women leaders such as

Elizabeth Cady Stanton and Susan B. Anthony centered their lobbying efforts on behalf of the suffrage movement in Congress (Simon and Danziger 1991). Women's hard-won fight for the right to vote and hold public office in the early 1900s, and later struggles for equality through the Women's Movement, set the stage for women's increased involvement in lobbying on the federal level throughout the twentieth century. Although women had been fighting for the passage of the Equal Rights Amendment (ERA) for fifty years prior to the 1970s, it was not until then that women's voice in the policy realm began to be taken seriously. Women's lobbying efforts on behalf of women's interests were taken so seriously that interest organizations began to mount a "strong backlash." According to Ryan (1979, 68), "The strong conservative response began in earnest after 1973, after the ERA passed Congress. STOP ERA was founded by Phyllis Schlafly in October of that year; likewise, the National Right to Life movement organized within a few months of the Supreme Court abortion decision." In addition to opposition from conservative groups, "women's interests" continued to be seen as in conflict with corporate interests. Following the well-known 1970 AT&T case, in which the company was found guilty of sex discrimination, "women's equality was seen as an expensive and threatening reality to corporate interests," and gave rise to conservative think tanks like the Heritage Foundation[2] (Ryan 1979, 68).

Nevertheless, the group consciousness and sisterhood women built centuries before laid the foundations for political activism. Women developed an instrumental conception of their gender, as individuals who are able to bring about social and political change through their actions and interactions (Cott 1977). By the mid–twentieth century women were fighting for their rights in the home, workplace, and political realm. With the Supreme Court ruling on *Roe vs. Wade* in 1973, women, as a group, came to be seen as force to be reckoned with. Since the 1960s, women have lobbied hard and won concessions on a whole range of women's issues, including sexual harassment, domestic violence, women's health and welfare, gun control, and animal rights. As women came to identify not only as wives and mothers, but also as paid workers, they have lobbied for equal treatment in the workplace. Through their participation in nongovernmental organizations (NGOs) in this country and around the world, women have mounted effective lobbying campaigns in the public interest. Over the last few centuries, women have won a public voice in the political realm. It has become acceptable for women to visibly protest, resist, and lobby for legislative change at the state and federal levels.

Depending on their brand of feminism, women have not always come down on the same side of the political fence around particular issues, as in the case of abortion. It is clear, however, that historically women's lobbying activity mostly centered on what are defined as women's issues, reflecting the interests of women as a group and conceptualized as mostly related to the private sphere—children, family, and home. It was not until the late twentieth century, when the proportion of managerial positions occupied by women and men finally reached parity, that there was a corresponding flow of women into the realm of corporate public relations and government relations (Donato 1990; Nownes and Freeman 1998; Schlozman and Tierney 1986). Women are now commonly seen fighting for the very corporate and government interests they historically fought against.

A SURGE IN WOMEN CORPORATE LOBBYISTS

Nownes and Freeman (1998) note that for most of American history, women have comprised less than 5 percent of active Washington lobbyists. Of *all* registered lobbyists at the state level, it is estimated that women now constitute approximately a third. In a study of Washington lobbyists, Bath et al. find that women comprise 35 percent of their sample (n=211). Although still falling short of parity, they certainly no longer stand out as an anomaly on the lobbying scene. According to a survey conducted by the Foundation for Public Affairs, the research arm of the Public Affairs Council, there has been a jump of 13 percent over the last three years in the number of corporations with Washington offices. Correspondingly, the number of Washington lobbyists is more than double the number recorded five years ago (Public Affairs Council 2005). Women's entrance into corporate-government affairs contributes significantly to these growing numbers.

Men still far outnumber women among the top "hired guns." Hired guns can be characterized as "high-priced, well regarded, 'super lobbyists,'" who work for lobbying, public re-lations, and law firms in Washington (Nownes and Freeman 1998). However, women have made some degree of headway in recent years. For example, there is Susan Hirshman, former chief of staff and adviser to House Republican leaders, and Su-san Molinari, a former Republican congresswoman who heads a prominent Washington lobbying and PR firm. Among the top hired guns identified in a recent article in the *Hill* (2005) is also Linda Daschle, of Daschle, Baker, Donelson, Bearman, Caldwell & Berkowitz, who lobbies the Senate in the wake of her hus-band's loss. Probably most prominent among women who are top "hired guns" in Washington is Anne Wexler, of Wexler and Walker Public Policy Associates. Since her stint as top policy ad-visor in the Carter administration three decades ago, Wexler has been a "fixture on K Street"[3] (Cusak et al. 2005).

While women have not yet significantly infiltrated the world of "hired guns" in Washington, they have made great strides in lobbying and other government relations positions *within* corporations and business trade associations. Most of the analysis for this book is therefore concentrated on this group. Government relations operations within corporations have grown rapidly in the last few decades (Donato 1990; Scott

1991; Schlozman and Tierney 1986). Women's entrance into corporate lobbying contributes significantly to this growth. The number of women who work as lobbyists and other corporate-government affairs positions within corporations increased by over 100 percent during the 1980s[4] and continues to grow at a fast pace, corresponding with the more general movement of women into professional and managerial occupations and surpassing women's movement into other areas of the economy (Blum and Smith 1988; Jacobs 1995; Kaufman 1989; Reskin and Phipps 1988; Wagman and Folbre 1988).

Women who lobby for top corporations in Washington generally occupy high-paid, highly visible, well-connected, and potentially influential positions within and outside the corporation (Scott 1991, 1996). The average annual pay for a federal corporate government relations official in 2000 was $138,963, over twice that of men in all managerial positions (U.S. Bureau of the Census 2000). Although still underrepresented at the very top of the organizational hierarchy within corporate government affairs, women increasingly hold the prestigious titles of manager, director, and, ever more commonly, vice president of corporate government affairs. Many of the women in these positions are registered lobbyists. Others do not call themselves lobbyists, but nevertheless spend a majority of their time interacting with legislators and staffers with regard to policy issues of interest to their corporations or business as a whole or both. During the 1980s, the number of women government relations managers increased five-fold, vice presidents six-fold, and directors almost nine-fold. There was also a sizable increase in the proportions of women in these categories, with women occupying almost 25 percent of all manager positions, 19 percent of all directors, and 5 percent of all vice-president positions. By 1995, these proportions more than doubled, with women occupying half of all manager positions, and a third of all director positions. In the early 1980s, Bendix's Nancy Reynolds was the only woman among the heads of top corporations' Washington offices. Among all corporations with Washington offices, women made up only 5 percent of government relations vice presidents. By 1995, at least a quarter of all corporate government relations operations in Washington, D.C., were headed by women (*Washington Representatives,* annual editions). Moreover, women are increasingly found representing all areas of the economy in the legislative realm, from mining and trucking to financial industries. They specialize in a wide range of policy areas. There is no doubt women have made enormous strides in the area of corporate lobbying over the last few decades.

What Is a Lobbyist?

There are at least 35,000 *registered* lobbyists in Washington, according to reports, but this figure significantly underestimates the amount of influence peddling that takes place in the nation's capital for at least two reasons. First, lobbying laws are complicated, so enforcement becomes difficult. It is also easier for those who are noncompliant to build a case around the argument that they just "didn't understand the rules." In his response to questions concerning his, and his fellow legislators' involvement in the Jack Abramoff lobbying scandal, Tom DeLay, former Senate majority whip, responded, "I think most members have done things on what they understand to be the up and up. They may not understand the rules, which are very confusing" (Allen 2005, A5). Second, there are many ways for those on both sides of the fence—lobbyists and government officials—to get around the rules.

According to the Lobbying Disclosure Act of 1995, a "lobbying contact" is defined as: "any oral, written, or electronic communication to a covered official that is made on behalf of a client with regard to the enumerated subjects at 2 U.S.C. 2602 (8) (B)." "Enumerated subject" refers to a list of policy areas provided. "Lobbying activities" are "lobbying contacts and nay efforts in support of such contracts, including preparation or planning activities, research and other background work that is intended, at the time of its preparation, for use in contacts and coordination with the lobbying activities of others." A "lobbyist" is defined as "any individual who (1) is either employed or retrained by a client for financial or other compensation (2) for services that include more than one lobbying contact; and (3) whose lobbying activities constitute twenty percent or more of his or her services on behalf of that client during any six-month period." Organizations, such as corporations, employing in-house lobbyists file a single registration. An organization is exempt from registration if its total expenses for lobbying activities do not exceed and are not expected to exceed $24,500 during a semiannual period.

Federal lobbyists are required to file semiannual reports, which contain the following areas of disclosure: general lobbying issue areas, specific issue area, House and federal agencies contacted, disclosure of lobbyists who have activity in general areas, and description of interest of foreign entity (if applicable). Generally, registration requirements at the state level are more stringent than at the federal level (Broder 2006). According to The Center for Public Integrity (2003), many states require reports to be submitted every month, much more frequently than at the federal level. States require more detailed itemization of spending. Federal lobbyists are not required to register until forty-five days after performing duties considered lobbying activities or have been contracted to perform lobbying activities, whereas in at least twenty states lobbyists are required to register prior to performing any activity. In another seventeen states, lobbyists are required to report within the first five days.

In the aftermath of Washington scandals involving high-powered lobbyists and their allies in business and government, there was a barrage of House and Senate proposals to tighten federal lobbying rules, including more frequent (quarterly) reporting, more restriction on and disclosure of gift giving, and tighter revolving door rules such as a longer "cooling off period before a legislator or government official can become a lobbyist," and one proposal to bar former government officials from the House gym. Some lobbyists were defensive. "We all have our bad apples, and Jack Abramoff is ours," said Paul Miller, president of the American League of Lobbyists (Broder 2006, A1). But many legislators panicked. "They were scared to death they would go back home and people would be waiting as they got off the plane with buckets of tar and bales of feathers," says Professor James Thurber of American University (Stolberg 2006a, A1). Only hours after Jack Abramoff was sentenced to almost six years in prison for his dubious lobbying practices, the Senate overwhelmingly passed the first major lobbying restriction legislation in over a decade (Stolberg 2006b). The restrictions were mostly on gifts and travel, rules for disclosing information on pet projects, and frequency of reporting.

Critics argue that the new, tighter, restrictions are a "smoke screen," and do little to curb the disproportionate power of lobbyists, and the interests they represent, in Washington. This is particularly the case for corporate lobbyists, primarily because representatives of business and government view themselves as allies, even family, in the policy arena to begin with. They frequent the same social clubs, attend the same events, go to the same restaurants, and generally share a social world. Corporations get around lobbying restrictions by forming business–government organizations or coalitions, like the Republican Main Street Partnership, an alliance of lawmakers, staffers, and lobbyists. The lobbyists pay $25,000 to have 3 lunch briefings with lawmakers, and VIP seating for eight at a black-tie dinner for the coalition. Non-profit advocacy groups like the Main Street Partnership "can seek unlimited and undisclosed corporation donations" because it is organized as such a group (Kirkpatrick 2006, A26). As critics point out, "all these moderate Republicans who support all this campaign finance and lobbying reform have this convoluted organization that basically raises a variety of corporate funding and apparently pays for pajama parties with lobbyists" (Kirkpatrick 2006, A26). Republicans are not the only ones who belong to such business-government coalitions. The Tax Coalition is an organization that includes both business and government representatives, both Democrat and Republican, as members. Although the public sector members pay only a small membership fee, they are nevertheless considered full-fledged members of the organization and also serve on the event planning committee. Many of the members of these business-government coalitions and organizations are not registered lobbyists. In fact, even if they are, they wouldn't want to be called lobbyists. In an editorial in the *St. Louis Post-Dispatch* in 2005, Robert McDonald of Emerson Electric says, "Lobbyists don't like to be called lobbyists. The men and women of K Street in Washington prefer to think that they're educating members of Congress. At Emerson, we never use the term 'lobby.'" Nor do they call their organizations as lobbying organizations, but rather places where business and government officials exchange information and educate each other.

THE JOB: MAKING CONNECTIONS

What do corporate lobbyists do in their jobs? In the most general terms, corporate lobbyists and other government relations officials are responsible for keeping track of what the government is doing or considering doing. They must also know what's going on within the corporation, and in other corporations, in order to know which issues to follow and who to contact for advice. Reactions are elicited from various people inside and outside the corporation in order to find out whether a law or regulation poses problems, and whether changes would make it easier for the company to live with them. The government relations person then lobbies to get the change enacted through appropriate government channels, whether Congress or a regulatory agency (Scott 1996). As in other occupations, building networks provides access to key people. Who you know is often as important as what you know (Brass 1992; Granovetter 1973; Smith-Lovin and McPherson 1993; Wellman et al. 1988). Nowhere are connections more important than in lobbying. My survey data indicate that both women and men government relations officials are well connected to those in business and government.

Fundraisers

Fundraisers provide a good illustration of the contexts within which government relations managers establish connections and the significance of these connections. The vast majority of government relations officials surveyed (94 percent) attend fundraisers. Most report that fundraisers are a good place to mingle with key people in business and government. As one woman lobbyist notes:

> Basically you try to go physically and be at as many as you can, because then you get to see them (legislators) and thank them for their work for you, and they see you. They know that you're supporting them, you meet other people there, and they have an opportunity to discuss issues. I went to three yesterday, and one last night. We've never given to this congressman before, and I don't know him well at all. We talked about ten minutes and then I met and talked to the staff person who was there that I work with, and I talked with her about twenty minutes on issues that were important to us. So there was time very well spent.

Women are almost as likely as men to attend fundraisers, according to survey results. Ninety-three percent of women, compared with ninety-seven percent of men, say they attend. There are several ways, or conditions under which, fundraisers might be considered particularly useful for women lobbyists. Women's presence at fundraisers may provide an opportunity to elevate their status—to be recognized as an active and significant part of the political process:

> I give a lot of counsel to young women, coming off the Hill going to corporations or negotiating jobs. I feel one of the most important things, especially as a woman, that you can do is insure that you are the one who is representing your company at fundraisers. Because as long as we don't have public financing of campaigns, members' political futures depend on raising money. Then you are seen as the one who is helping them on their fundraising campaigns. You are no longer just a servant. You are no longer the note-taker. You have more credibility. So I think it is very important. It's an integral part of how this city [Washington] operates.

Corporations often use the fundraiser as an occasion to present the contribution check, rather than inviting the candidate to their company or mailing it to them. Since corporations use the contribution as a tool to develop and solidify relationships with legislators and staff members, if women deliver the check it follows that they would have greater access to these people.

One woman government relations manager notes that the "ideal" situation is to hand the check over personally at the fundraiser: "The preference is that the check be there and taken to the fundraiser. Having worked on the Hill, I know the day after a fundraiser you count all the checks, and you kind of want to be in that pile. That's the ideal. What I insist on is that we have a letter that goes with every check. The check may say '[subsidiary name] PAC' or '[parent company name] PAC.'"

How often do women deliver checks? According to the mail survey, in offices where the respondent is a woman, women deliver the check 43 percent of the time. In offices where the respondent is a man, women deliver the check only 12 percent of the time. Because the survey does not ask the number of women in these offices, this question does not provide a truly accurate measure. But we at least know that in cases where there is a woman respondent there is at least one woman government relations manager in the office. In these cases, women appear to be more than tokens; rather, they are a substantial proportion of those representing the company with contributions in hand.

The size of the fundraiser is an important factor in determining the level and character of interaction with those in business and government. Small gatherings are typically preferred over large affairs. Some government relations managers make a special effort to arrive early, while the crowd is still small, allowing them to spend more time with the legislator or staff member. Says one corporate woman, "I like to get there when it starts because the member, whoever is hosting, is usually there at the beginning. And before the crowd gets there, you have a chance to kind of talk with him, and once the mob gets there it's like a receiving line."

Likewise, small breakfasts or receptions attended by a legislator or staff person and perhaps several representatives of corporations provide government relations managers a better opportunity to be noticed and to present their cases than large fundraisers, described as "cattle shows" by one interviewee: "They are for the most part what we call cattle shows that we are obligated to attend. In general they are receptions in the evening or sometimes they are small breakfasts, but for the most part they are huge extravaganza kinds of things where you have maybe three hundred or four hundred people attending. You are lucky if you get to even say 'hi' to the member. You just go up and have a glass of wine and some hors d'oeuvres."

Men may be more advantaged than women by virtue of the character of the fundraisers they attend. A higher proportion of men than women report attending small (under twenty people) fundraisers, although the difference is not statistically significant. According to the interviews, however, women stress the importance of attending small gatherings, and that they aim to do so, as often as men:

> The smaller they are, the more intimate they are, the more worthwhile an effort it is; the bigger they are and the broader the interests that show up, you get no return at all on even showing up for it. But I think what we try to do is get them tied more directly to our industry at the very least. Today we had one—it was a fundraiser for paper industry lobbyists. I'll meet with this one member of Congress, and there will probably be ten people there, companies represented. And we had a fundraiser for this member of Congress, and for two hours he talked about the paper industry and our interests, things that were going on, investments we're making and that sort of thing. That's a real worthwhile effort.

There is some evidence from the interviews that the structure and culture of fundraising is changing. As a government relations manager for a top corporation said:

> It is very interesting to see how the Washington culture has changed over the past twenty years or so. It has gone from being an entirely male-dominated city, entirely from a three-martini lunch kind of stuff ... I don't think it is limited to our industry, but we try do much more focused kind of things. You know, get people from the same industry sit around the table at either breakfast or lunch or dinner so that you can talk about stuff and so that you are not pulling a legislator fifty million ways. You can actually educate them about something and have a nice time—because fundraising has to be the biggest drag for people. It must be awful, so you try to make it as pleasant an experience as possible.

Examined more closely in chapter 5, this change in the fundraising culture may be driven, at least in part, by women's work and family ties. As more women with family responsibilities occupy corporate lobbying positions, making large evening fundraisers difficult, we may see a shift to intimate breakfasts or lunches as a way for government relations representatives to present their check and, at the same time, get the ear of government officials.

Golfing, Shooting, a Week at the Spa

Fundraisers are not the only occasions where corporate lobbyists establish the relationships that are a significant part of their jobs, nor are they necessarily the most important. As voiced by male legislative aide, and echoed by other interviewees:

> There is a huge sort of golf culture up here [on Capitol Hill] where people can get out and establish relationships with one another without sitting and having a fifteen minute meeting. To a large extent, the golfing, most women don't play. I mean that's a whole area of networking that sort of excluded them unless they took up the game. But, I mean, I don't think men would necessarily say to a woman, "Oh, let me take you golfing." But they wouldn't hesitate to ask a man, thinking that they probably play because most guys up here do.

Although it is the case that the golf courses are still dominated by men, women have come to understand that exclusion from this "culture" is deleterious to them as corporate lobbyists and government officials. The Women's Congressional Golf Association (WCGA) is a group of over 200 women lobbyists and staffers who feel that "golf is more than just a sport or a pastime to members of the lobbying profession ... it's a business tool that allows them a unique opportunity to get cozy with Members of Congress, their aides, potential clients and their fellow lobbyists" (Ackley 2005, 1). According to LeeAnn Petersen, corporate government relations manager for Volvo Group North America, the WCGA was formed because women lobbyists realized that,

"Golf is essential to business, particularly if you're a woman. Men get those types of opportunities all the time. As a woman, if you want a seat at the table . . ." (Ackley 2005, 1).

Still, some women lobbyists argue that the golf course is "pretty much male turf." According to Martha Burk, a leader in fighting for women's admittance to the Augusta National Golf Club, "In the nineteenth century, men and women played golf together. But in the twentieth century, the culture of golf took a sexist turn." About twenty-five golf clubs in the United States still do not admit women as members. And even when women are present on the course, says Burk, "I don't think that a woman by and large is going to be viewed as an equal in a golf foursome" (Ackley 2005, 2).

Another group of women lobbyists have found that a day of shooting small orange saucers with twenty-gauge shotguns is "a delightful way to bond" (Rothstein 2005, 21). The Washington Women's Shooting Club was established eleven years ago by two lobbyists, Suzie Brewster and Bess Conway. More than 100 women participate in 6-week leagues all during the year. Shooting has always been popular among men on Capitol Hill as a way to connect. Now that women want to be part of the "club," they are taking up the sport as well. Megan McChesney, a lobbyist with the conservative Americans for Tax Reform, convinced her boss to let her attend the "Fall Girls and Guns Shoot" of the WWSC. She had no problem persuading him since he sits on the NRA board.

Many of the members of the Women's Shooting Club say that they have never had, nor will they ever have, the desire to shoot a living thing. As they stand in line, waiting for their chance to shoot, they talk about how sad they feel when they accidentally run over squirrels with their cars. But some admit that, given time, they may be up to the task. As Beth Hellmann says, "Who knows? I'll be out there in ten years shooting deer" (Rothstein 2005, 21) Among the women interviewees for this book, several mentioned joining Washington, D.C., hunting clubs as a way to infiltrate the Washington "old boys network."

Women lobbyists also network with each other through membership in professional and policy organizations. Half of the women surveyed report that they belong to work-related organizations composed of women in their field. There are trade organizations, such as Women in Mining and Women in Finance, policy organizations such as the Tax Coalition and the Secure Retirement Coalition, and professional organizations such as Women in Government Affairs. These organizations typically hold regular meetings and events in Washington, D.C. Some hold annual "retreats," where their members engage in activities such as golf, tennis, and soaking in the spa. Organizational membership provides women lobbyists with an environment in which to share job information, advice, and establish connections with other women in corporations, trade associations, and government.

More generally, and overwhelmingly the case in Washington, women government relations managers share a social world on a day-to-day basis with their male and female colleagues and those in government: "You run into these people all the time. You run into them at the grocery store, these members of Congress that you're talking to. Last summer I was taking our babysitter home. I had my four-year old in the back of the car and we're driving down the street, Sunday night at 9:30. There's nobody on the road, and my car dies. I think, 'What am I going do?' This guy pulls up; I look at his license plate. He's a Congressman on the House Ways and Means Committee. He's a guy I still see from time to time. He helped me out." They frequent the same restaurants, athletic organizations, and hair salons, as illustrated by one corporate lobbyist who said, "I was getting my hair done a couple of weeks ago, and I had a very early appointment. I was amazed by the women in the shop—a number of well-known, well-connected, high-placed, high-powered women—and a lot of talk was going on. One of them, a woman I know, said, 'Oh yes, I get a lot of work done here in the mornings.'"

It is by being part of this common culture that individuals form important bonds and hear about career opportunities as well as various other kinds of information important for their jobs. One corporate lobbyist said, when talking about participating in business or political groups, "They turn into almost a little bit social, or you feel like it because you are seeing these people a lot, but they really do give you some information that you need to do your job."

ARE WOMEN LOBBYISTS DIFFERENT?

We know very little about attitudinal or behavioral differences between women and men lobbyists of any kind, much less corporate lobbyists. In one of the few existing studies in this area, Nownes and Freeman (1998, 1194–1195) find that, at the state level, women lobbyists are "taken as seriously" as men, measured primarily by the frequency with which they are "approached for advice." In fact, when controlling for various factors, including experience, education, and group type, women tend to be approached much more frequently than men by policymakers. Likewise, Bath et al. (2005, 144–145) find that, although women and men use the same "techniques," women are "substantially more likely than men to be approached for advice frequently." They also find that women and men lobbyists have "very similar levels of access to executive agencies," while women "interact with fewer legislative committees" than do men (Bath et al., 2005, 146).

With regard to corporate lobbyists' networking in particular, my own research shows some gender differences. For instance, women corporate government relations officials are more likely than their male counterparts to interact with legislative staff than members of Congress. They are particularly more likely than men to interact with women staffers. Men, on the other hand, are more likely than women to attend social events with members of Congress, such as having meals and attending sporting events and concerts. Although the character of their connections differs in some ways, my research shows that both men and women who represent corporations are heavily entrenched in the lobbying scene.

Perhaps more significant than the actual differences by gender in behaviors and attitudes is the fact that women lobbyists *believe* they are different, and that the differences are somehow "natural." During my observation of the Tax Alliance retreat, a woman who is counsel to the Senate Finance Committee explained at dinner one evening that women and men approach things differently, and how this is "proven" in books, film, and other media. "Women are still gathering," she said emphatically. She gave an example of a TV advertisement, where a "bunch of people" are watching a football game. There is a bowl of chips on the table. "Each guy takes one," and they do this repeatedly until they are all gone. "One guy figures he brought the beer, the other the chips, so they leave getting more chips to the last guy who waits to get them until a break in the game. Women, on the other hand, who are watching the game, will see that there are no (or few) chips left, and all go to get more collectively. That's how men and women are different." Similarly, Mary Ruble, in-house lobbyist for Ameritech, argues that women take a more collective and less "confrontational" approach to lobbying: "Women bring some very good qualities to the lobbying arena . . . Women are skilled at bringing people together in order to reach an understanding of different viewpoints . . . We're peacemakers, preferring a path away from conflict and confrontations" (Carr-Elsing 1999, 1). Likewise, Lynn Padovan, executive director of the Illinois Environmental Council, says, "Women are great mediators and facilitators . . . I think we're naturals" (Nickel 2000, 1). Others argue that women are more effective at lobbying because they are more honest and moralistic than men.

Most of the "natural," "innate" differences between women and men described by women lobbyists reflect and reinforce the expressive-instrumental dichotomy that has served to justify gender inequality since the rise of capitalism. Women are expected and assumed to be peaceful, nurturing, trustworthy, and honest relative to men. They are viewed as inherently less confrontational, more nurturing, better at "expressive" interaction work. These expectations are clearly reflected in the way women lobbyists characterize themselves in relation to men, and they are not alone. Male lobbyists use similar terms to characterize their female counterparts. Former Representative Bill Brewster, who teaches a course at the Fall Girls Shoot Out, says, "Women have a different attitude. Women are more supportive of each other" (Rothstein 2005, 21).

On the other hand, the women and men interviewed for the book report that lobbying increasingly involves much more than simply schmoozing. In addition to being good at interacting with key people in business and government, lobbyists must also "know their information." This is true now more than ever, as Mary Ruble explains: "The sharing of information is important in the political process nowadays because issues are very complex ... People need to know that they can believe you and trust the information that you're giving them" (Carr-Elsing 1999, 2). According to many of the women interviewed, women lobbyists are better than men at knowing the specific information needed to be effective in their jobs. That this perception is generally held by key people in business and government is evidenced by the finding of Nownes and Freeman (1998) mentioned earlier that women lobbyists are more likely than men to be approached for advice. It is not necessarily the case that women are seen as natural at aspects of the job that are characterized as "instrumental" (obtaining and knowing technical information) versus "expressive" (interacting, nurturing, peacemaking). However, if women are viewed as effective at this increasingly valued part of the job (perhaps even more effective than their male counterparts), they are more likely to be taken seriously within their organizations. At the same time, conceptions of government relations work on the whole, relative to other kinds of work, are slow to change.

THE BOTTOM LINE

Corporate lobbyists, and government affairs operations more generally, help companies save billions of dollars each year by influencing policy decisions, and thereby contribute greatly to the corporation's ability to accumulate profit. That government relations work does, in fact, contribute to the accumulation of wealth and profit, is articulated by government relations officials. One woman notes: "To run this office on a yearly basis, pay the rent, and take care of all that stuff . . . the line manager who is looking at what is being sold and what it's costing him to sell and what his profits are in between. If you look at corporate affairs, public affairs, we are not a moneymaking operation. But people like us in Washington save money for the corporation. If we win on this [regulatory] thing, it's $6 million for the company."

Although the government relations operations, and women's lobbying efforts more specifically, clearly affect the company's bottom line, this area within the corporation is generally devalued relative to others because, unlike those of line or business managers, it is not seen as "instrumentally task oriented." Government relations work is more likely to be viewed as "schmoozing," involving more "emotion work" than instrumental labor. It is the case that, along with researching the issues, government relations officials must constantly engage in emotion work to maintain positive relations with government officials, representatives of other companies and trade associations, and the public. In doing so, they contribute "instrumentally" to the corporation's bottom line. But as long as this aspect of their work is characterized as "emotional" or "soft" or both, it will continue be seen as difficult to measure, and therefore devalued relative to other work. One government relations manager echoed the sentiments of others when she said, "There is a sense of 'I don't know what those people do. There must be all the booze parties.' There's also a sense of—we are not a profit center; we do not make money, we cost money."

However, women are very much aware of their function as corporate lobbyists and the valuation of their operations and actively attempt to make others in the corporation aware of the bottom-line effect of their contributions, through news-letters, presentations, and other means. One corporate govern-ment relations official spoke of using her company's employee communications department to bring about this awareness. She said, "We try to spend time going out to our employees, where we have pockets of employees and give them presentations on what is our agenda. Through our Employee Communications Department we try to do a news story occasionally that talks about a battle."

Ghiloni's phrase "the velvet ghetto" captures the dual char-acter of corporate-government affairs (Ghiloni 1987). On one hand, like other areas where women are concentrated within organizations, such as personnel and public relations, it can be-come a ghetto for women. On the other hand, it may offer cer-tain advantages. In addition to providing women with high sala-ries and prestigious titles relative to others in the labor force, it may offer them an opportunity to redefine the character of their work, potentially leading to greater power within the corpora-tion (Scott 1996).

Survey results show that women are significantly more likely than their male colleagues to report that women's sala-ries are worse than those of men. There is evidence from the interviews that women are not only aware of inequalities in compensation and valuation of their work, but also the broader processes by which women get ahead. A comment made by one corporate lobbyist best illustrates this point. She said, "The problem is, you still need to know and be able to move successfully within the white male power structure to be successful/accepted in the field. We need to be vigilant in the area of pay, benefits, titles, to ensure the field isn't downgraded due to the influx of female government relations officers."

Not only are women aware of the obstacles, but they also seem to be actively contesting existing arrangements in various ways. For instance, according to the survey data, women are significantly more likely than men to report that they had approached a superior asking that women receive higher salaries. Not only are women struggling to be equally compensated, but there is also evidence that they are working to redefine the character of their positions though developing a company-wide consciousness of their contribution to the bottom line.

One of the most important and visible committees in corporate-government affairs is the PAC Committee. The PAC Committee is the body responsible for making and approving recommendations concerning contributions to candidates. It is typically composed of between five and eight people. Although women are not as likely as men to be on the PAC Committee, and are far less likely to act as chair, there is evidence that they are not insignificant in the decision-making structure within government affairs. Survey data show that they are an important force in decisions about who sits on the committee, and thus in transforming the decision-making structure of government affairs. They are also powerful in the sense that they make decisions about contributions that are rarely challenged by company executives. There is further qualitative evidence that suggests women are pushing for increased involvement in the formal decision-making structure of government affairs and the corporation. One woman lobbyist for a top pharmaceutical company reports: "I am at this point the highest-ranking woman in corporate affairs. There are maybe about six women that make

more money than me. Traditionally, you just don't find women
in the [top] jobs. It's very sad. That's been one of my big com-
plaints. I made a comment to the Chairman [of the Board] one
time, when we lost a board member who had died suddenly of a
heart attack—'I hope you get a woman for that job.'"

Women may be in key positions, as corporate lobbyists, to
transform their conditions. Networks with men and women
on legislative staffs and in other companies enhance women's
opportunities and influence legislative or regulatory outcomes.
Networks with other women are particularly important in providing an environment for sharing common grievances and vital
information. Perhaps more significantly, they provide the basis
for a shared gender consciousness and political action. Bookman
and Morgen (1988) note that women understand and counter
patriarchal dominance as they organize around issues that are
not solely women's issues. The Tax Alliance (examined in chapter 4) is an example of how women in government affairs become empowered through their connections with other women
in business and government. The organization was formed primarily in response to women's exclusion from men's tax groups.
Women recognized their limitations as gender-based and took
action to change their circumstances.

At the same time, women's relatively recent entry into corporate lobbying and the networks they establish are significant
in advancing corporate interests, and corporate heads realize
this. Women lobbyists are a "better buy" than men lobbyists.
Women in government affairs earn significantly less than men,
controlling for years of experience, age, and education. Women
are thus a cheaper supply of government affairs labor than men,
and corporations are most likely aware of the costs of not hiring women. As more women move into positions on legislative staffs, particularly in policy areas where they were once
excluded (such as taxes, social security, and defense), hiring
women into government affairs positions is likely to be seen as

a way to ensure positive business–government relations, and thus help corporations achieve their political goals. As one woman corporate lobbyist notes: "There are a lot of women who are moving up on Capitol Hill, and I think there's a tie-in that could possibly be made around why more women are getting into government affairs. I think they're being hired because there are more women in these positions on Capitol Hill—not the elected members, but their staffs, where a lot of the decisions are made. And I think that corporations feel that if they have women, they can go in and talk to their women staffers more easily."

As women network with other women in corporations and trade associations and on legislative staffs, whether over lunch or at the theater, not only do they exert influence over legislative outcomes, but they also share a common culture which potentially makes it easier to communicate, establish trust, and do business (Kanter 1977; Zweigenhaft 1987). Hence, it would not be surprising if corporations were to continue to hire women to do their lobbying in the future.

But there is another, perhaps unintended, side to women's experiences and connections. Although government relations may be a "velvet ghetto" for women, and corporations may benefit from women's networks, nonetheless women corporate lobbyists may be empowered though their positions and connections inside and outside the corporation. Women in government affairs, like women in other fields who have entered the ranks of management, appear to be managers in fact and not just title (Jacobs 1995). Moreover, women's networks foster an awareness of a whole range of issues and information. Like ties formed by women through their participation in moral reform societies during the 1800s, one of the most significant aspects of the ties formed by women in business and government is that they provide the opportunity to develop a gender consciousness and willingness to struggle for their interests as women and as corporate political professionals. Most of the women in this study indicate that they are aware of, and struggle for, equity in pay and title; more than this, they are working to redefine women's work and women's power. Awareness of, and political action around, issues of inequality are potentially rooted in women's networks.

Women's power is inextricably linked to the corporate and patriarchal structures in which their positions and relations are embedded. As long as women act and interact within oppressive economic and political structures that devalue and inhibit, there will be barriers to women's struggles for power. But it is also the case that their positions in the corporate and political structure potentially provide both an awareness of the need for change, and a structural location to make change possible (Scott 1996). The following chapter looks more closely at the relationship between women's entry into corporate lobbying, women's interests, and corporate power.

CHAPTER 3

The Problem with No Name?

WOMEN'S INTERESTS, CORPORATE POWER, AND PUBLIC POLICY

ALTHOUGH STILL A relatively small proportion of all women lobbyists, there has been a recent increase in the number of those who specialize in policy areas traditionally thought of as "male," most notably tax and social security policy. At the same time, tax policy and social security policy increasingly advantages business to the detriment of other groups, most notably women. This chapter examines the contradictory positions of women corporate lobbyists who increasingly work in the interest of corporations through the passage of legislation that is contrary to the interests of women.

Women who specialize in tax and social security policy are no longer an anomaly in business and government. They lobby for top corporations and work as aides to legislators who serve on key tax-writing committees. A few have even served as top presidential advisors. One of the most successful and prominent of these women is Leanne Abdnor, who was commissioned by George W. Bush in 2001 to study the so-called funding problems facing social security. She appeared with Bush on the campaign trail, standing alongside him onstage, in support of his push for personal accounts. In 1995, Abdnor served as vice president of external affairs at Cato, a conservative nonprofit research foundation based in Washington, D.C., where she was "introduced to the gospel of privatization" (Vieth 2005). After Cato, Abdnor went to work for the Alliance for Worker Retirement Security, an organization created by the National Association of Manufacturers (the largest industrial trade organization in the United States) to promote private retirement accounts.

Within corporations, the number of women government relations officials who specialize in taxes and social security is also steadily increasing, as evidenced by the fact that many top U.S. firms such as Exxon, Pfizer, and American Express now employ women as their head legislative liaisons in the area of tax policy. As more and more women enter these policy areas, they are beginning to form networks, both formal and informal. Among women who lobby for corporate interests, and those who work crafting legislation and regulations in the government realm, organizations have sprung up to provide a place for women to share career and policy information and develop and maintain friendships. The Tax Alliance, examined in the next chapter, is one such organization, composed of women who represent top U.S. companies and women who work as legislative staffers and on congressional committees (such as the House Ways and Means), all of whom specialize in tax policy.

As growing numbers of women lobbyists enter what are typically viewed as "male" policy areas, policy is increasingly crafted to the advantage of business and, conversely, to the disadvantage of women and other groups. Public policy is not value-free; it reflects and maintains the interests of dominant groups and the ideologies that reinforce these interests. For instance, Heberle (1999) argues that homicide laws work to the disadvantage of women because inherent in them are assumptions about masculinity and femininity, such that "when women commit violence in the private sphere, they are breaking the rules of gender and must be either refeminized ... or severely sanctioned. When men commit violence in the private sphere, they are in a sense fulfilling the grim assumptions about masculinity. They do not have to be remasculinized to be considered redeemable or 'human.' Instead, judgment turns on whether they took masculinity too far" (Heberle 1999, 1103). The gendered nature of homicide policy helps explain why women, compared with men, receive harsher sentences, particularly when convicted of domestic homicide. Instead of being an engine for equality, state policy over time has increasingly become an engine for inequality.

This is true particularly in the case of tax and social security policy. In the United States, relative to other countries, tax and social security policy reflect and perpetuate an increasingly unequal distribution of power and wealth. Changes in tax rates, loopholes in the tax law, and proposals for privatized retirement accounts result in a system whereby the rich and powerful pay less and less (and in some cases zero) in taxes, while the working poor and middle class, and especially women, are held increasingly responsible and accountable for shouldering the burden.

It Wasn't Always This Way

"Taxation is not just the act of collecting revenues." Tax regimes are politically and economically driven, and usually "part of a larger schema of economic growth and redistribution in society" (Alexander 2000, 61). Back in 1913, the tax regime reflected the idea that "the basic means of sustaining life would not be taxed." Thus, capital was much more heavily taxed than income from wages "in the belief that is was morally offensive to take more from money earned by the sweat of one's brow than from money obtained by clipping coupons" (Johnston 2003, 19). Only "surplus" income was taxed, meaning that the tax regime at the time applied only to the economic elite. When World War I came around, taxes on the economic elite, such as the estate tax and the gift tax, were expanded. While income taxes on regular citizens also expanded, most people in the United States were still exempt from paying anything into the tax system (Johnston 2003).

After World War I, things changed dramatically. Gone were the days of placing the burden of funding wars, building roads, and improving technology on those who earn a "surplus" income. The mass now increasingly shared responsibility for the running of society. In 1924, the gift tax was imposed and, just prior to that, the estate tax. Before World War II, as a result of "New Deal politicking," Roosevelt made, as part of his political rhetoric, "fair" tax allocation a key issue. The 1935 Revenue Act, to "check the concentration of wealth," established new graduated rates on corporate income, and enacted other measures. In funding the defense program, he warned, "No one . . . should try, or be allowed, to get rich out of this program" (Alexander 2000, 64). Simultaneously, during the 1930s, in order to protect business from the New Deal reforms and labor movement challenges, corporations began to hire more public relations employees to convince the public that "what is good for General Motors is good for America" (Clawson et al. 1992, 154; Donato 1990, 131). Although legislation, such as the 1942 Revenue Act, raised corporate taxes and the excess profits tax from 60 percent to 90 percent, it was ridden with loopholes in favor of business, as business–government connections strengthened at the onset of World War II. At the same time, the income tax was further expanded and soon applied to all Americans.

The period after World War II saw an expansion in corporations' public affairs efforts. Nine out of ten businesses increased their expenditures in the area of public relations in 1946 (Donato 1990, 131). Corporations targeted employees, the public, and the government. Since the 1940s, there has been a steady increase in corporate government relations officials. Although "lobbying" is still a word that government relations officials are reluctant to use to describe themselves, by the 1970s and 1980s it was recognized as a subspecialty of public relations within corporations. Women also began to enter the field, in part so that corporations could advertise their affirmative action policies (Donato 1990).

Along with the increase in corporate lobbyists, beginning in the 1970s ordinary people found themselves assuming a greater and greater proportion of the income tax burden as there occurred a bracket creep, meaning that they were moved into higher tax brackets even though their real incomes remained unchanged (Johnston 2003, 20). Similarly, social security taxes, which once provided for a pay-as-you-go system that ensured a secure source of income in old age for the mass of working people in our society, are now put away to pay benefits more than three decades into the future. The government promised that these monies would be put in a "lock box" for the payment of benefits down the road. As Johnston notes, however, these taxes are not locked away, but instead "spent to help finance tax cuts for the super rich that began in 1981" (Johnston 2003, 20). By the 1980s, the tax system had been flipped on its head, transformed from one that promoted an egalitarian distribution of resources, to one that shifts the burden off of the rich and onto ordinary taxpayers, thus creating and perpetuating economic inequality.

But it was not until the 1990s, just as the number of Washington corporate lobbyists was rising dramatically, that the tax burden on corporations and the super rich took a huge nosedive. "When the Bush tax cuts of 2001, 2002, and 2003 are fully in place in 2010, the share of taxes paid by the bottom 95 percent of taxpayers will rise by 3.8 percentage points, while for the top 5 percent it will fall by the same amount" (Johnston 2003, 96). Although corporate profits are growing faster than the incomes of ordinary citizens, the taxes paid by U.S. businesses are falling dramatically (Johnston 2000). Because of a growing ideology among those in regulatory agencies and government that profits should not be taxed, and because of a variety of shelters and other loopholes worked into various pieces of legislation, corporate taxes have recently dropped to their "lowest sustained level" as a share of the economy in decades. In 1965, corporate income tax made up 4.1 percent of the gross domestic product (GDP). By 2000, the percentage had dropped to 2.5 percent. At the same time, in European countries the percentage of corporate tax is increasing. The National Association of Manufacturers called a recent a piece of U.S. legislation "the largest business tax relief program in more than a decade" (Citizens for Tax Justice 2003, 2005).

Between 1996 and 2000, 60 percent of the large U.S. corporations paid no income tax at all. For four of five years between 1995 and 2000, General Motors paid no taxes, despite profits of over $12 billion. Colgate-Palmolive, which earned $1.6 million in profits, paid no taxes in three of those years (Citizens for Tax Justice 2002b). Some companies not only saved money, but reaped huge benefits during those tax-free years. From 1996 to 1998, forty-one companies paid less than zero in federal income taxes in at least one year. Instead of paying the government taxes at the 35 percent rate that large companies should pay, Texaco received $3.4 billion in U.S. profits and $304 million in rebates (Institute on Taxation and Economic Policy 2000). El Paso Energy received rebates of $254 million over a five-year period, at a tax rate of -15.5 percent (Citizens for Tax Justice 2002b).

Just as President Bush calls for tax cuts for ordinary citizens, new shelters for corporations, reductions in the capital gains tax, and new breaks for retirement savings are being introduced by Republican leaders (Mitchell 2001). Although the political rhetoric presents recent tax cuts as benefiting the poor and middle classes and functioning as a tool for stimulating the economy, those who actually reap the most benefit from these so-called cuts are the rich. Congressional leaders who advocate a "repeal of the death tax," for example, appeal to people's belief that the government should not be able to cut into the hard-earned dollars that they are entitled to pass along to their children, when, in fact, the "estate tax" affects only about 2 percent of Americans to whom this tax applies, and only a small proportion of these people actually pay it due to exemptions (Johnston 2006, C8;

2003, 75). Folbre (2001, 174) calls this the "stupidity tax," because most people who pay it "simply hadn't bothered to figure out how to avoid it."

The political language used by Bush and his allies in government, with the help of the popular media, leaves out an important piece of the tax story—that recent tax cuts for the mass are nothing compared with the tax breaks received by those at the top. In addition to tax relief through deferred compensation, billions of dollars are saved each year as a result of policies that affect taxation on stocks, offshore profits, charitable trusts, and capital investments, all of which benefit corporations and corporate heads. Accelerated depreciation rules allow for the write-off of capital investments faster than the assets actually wear out. Among the biggest beneficiaries of these rules is the petroleum industry. For example, one piece of legislation, H.R. 6, allows for certain natural gas pipelines to be completely depreciated over fifteen years, "far less than the actual useful life of such pipelines." The estimated ten-year cost of this legislation is $3.1 billion. The bill also lets certain "geological and geophysical costs associated with oil exploration" to be written off at a faster rate, costing another $1 billion (Citizens for Tax Justice 2005).

Offshore corporate tax-sheltering schemes are yet another way that the government subsidizes business at the expense of others. Increasingly, corporations declare foreign countries as their "tax homes," even though their corporate headquarters are in the United States. An example is the Bermuda tax-avoidance scheme, described by Pulitzer Prize–winning journalist David Cay Johnston as follows:

> Corporations are busy moving intellectual property such as patents, trademarks and the title to the company logo to entities organized in tax havens like Bermuda. These corporations then pay royalties to use their own intellectual property, allowing them to convert taxable profits in the United

States into tax-deductible payments sent to Bermuda and
other havens that impose little or no tax. You pay for this
through higher taxes, reduced services or your rising share
of our growing national debt. You also pay for it through
incentives in the tax system for companies to build new
factories and to reduce employment in America. (Johnston
2003, 14)

According to David Francis (1999), reporter with the *Christian
Science Monitor*, 67 percent of so-called "foreign-based" corporations are doing hundreds of billions of dollars worth of
business in the United States without paying a cent of U.S.
income taxes.

There are far too many corporate tax-avoidance schemes
embedded in governmental laws and regulations to cover in
detail for the purpose of this discussion. The key point is that,
although the Bush administration would love for us to believe
that we are getting huge tax breaks, recent changes in tax policy in reality serve to disproportionately benefit the corporate
elite. It is important to note that the same is true in the case
of social security policy, where changes proposed by the administration are presented as beneficial to the poor and middle
class when in fact they serve only to benefit those at the top. In
promoting privatized retirement accounts, for example, conser-
vatives in government call for raising the ceiling on favorable
tax treatment for individual accounts. In effect, this change will
most benefit those who have the most "surplus" dollars available for investment.

Social security policy, like deferred compensation and accelerated depreciation law, can be thought of as an economic
redistribution program. Social security taxes subsidize the rich
at the expense of everyone else. In response to the growing
concern over the inadequate funding of the social security account, workers in the United States are required to pay for the

future solvency of the program. Regardless of whether there is an actual social security crisis, the fact is that this is the only tax workers are required to pay in advance of the benefits they receive, if they ever receive them. The government was supposed to keep the extra social security taxes in a lock box so that money would be there for when people filed for their benefits. According to Johnston (2003, 125), President Bush picked the lock box and spent the money on war machinery and FBI operations and the running of the Environmental Protection Agency.

In recent times, taxes on social security wages have risen, taking more and more money out of the checks of workers who are struggling to make ends meet. Meanwhile, those who earn more than the maximum for the social security tax have more to spend or invest. In 2003, the government took 6.2 cents out of each dollar earned, but only up to $87,000. One way to look at this is that people who earn higher salaries "get a tax break on every additional dollar they earn" over and above this ceiling (Johnston 2003, 121).

Thus, tax and social security policies in the United States are not value-free, but reflect and perpetuate structures of power and wealth inequality. By "shifting the burden off the super rich and onto everyone else" (Johnston 2003, 17), and by doing so in ways that are not obvious or even visible to ordinary citizens, not only are ideologies of meritocracy and equality reproduced, but in practice even more money is put into the pockets of the super rich.

Helping Business and Screwing Everyone Else

The 2002 and 2003 tax bills increased corporate tax subsidies officially by $178 billion in the years 2002–2004. It is estimated that these breaks cost over $400 billion in tax revenue in a decade (Citizens for Tax Justice 2003b). This is a conservative estimate; the figure is suspected to be much larger. Some of the costs are hidden, because the provisions do not take effect until years into the future. The costs to society of tax relief for corporations and the rich are, in effect, dollars that could be put into savings or investment. The social security taxes not paid on incomes over the limit amounts to money in the pockets of individuals that can be spent or invested.

At the same time, income for those at the top has soared while those at the bottom struggle to keep up with the cost of inflation. The Institute for Policy Studies reports that if average pay for production workers had grown at the same rate as CEO pay since 1990, their 2000 annual earnings would have been $120,491 instead of $24,668. Minimum-wage workers would have been earning $25.50 instead of a measly $5.15 per hour. (Institute for Policy Studies 2001). This growing income inequality is made worse by legislation that lets the rich set aside an unlimited portion of their income for years without being taxed. While Congress holds ordinary people accountable for paying taxes on every penny of their income, corporate executives are allowed to put a portion of their income, untaxed, into investments that will make them even richer.

Tax and social security policy thus result in a redistribution of money and power. Increasingly, taxes paid by the poor and middle class not only subsidize corporations and the super rich, but make it almost impossible for many working people to pull themselves up the economic ladder. Tax and social security policy in the United States disadvantages the poor and middle class and contributes to the reproduction of inequality in two significant ways. First, corporate tax-avoidance schemes drain the Treasury of needed revenue to fund social programs while shifting the burden onto the working poor and middle class as corporate taxes have declined and rates on high-income earners have been reduced. As Folbre (2001, 174) says, we could raise $50 billion, like Japan, to build new preschools. Instead, in the United States, education, healthcare, and employment programs are deprived of funding as a result of growing welfare programs for the rich. Sociologists have long documented the ill effects of poor healthcare and education on opportunities to break out of the cycle of poverty and get ahead.

Second, as the working poor and middle class assume more of the tax burden, they are left with little, if any, money to spend, save, or invest. Many people will not be able to afford to put money into the private social security accounts proposed by President Bush, let alone make risky investments that will likely yield high dividends. The working poor are particularly vulnerable, since they barely earn even enough to pay for their subsistence. Deciding whether to buy milk for their children or put money into a retirement account, most would opt for the milk. Many are not covered by health insurance, and thus will have to face decisions of whether to repair a broken leg or damaged heart or put money into retirement. The working poor simply will not be able to take advantage of Bush's proposed private accounts. This means that many people will be forced to remain in the workforce well into old age. For those who have spent their lives employed in working-class jobs, many of which involve significant physical exertion, this would prove difficult if not impossible. When a Washington consultant attending the Tax Alliance retreat (where I conducted observation research) raised this very point during a morning session on social security and taxes, the corporate government affairs officials present were puzzled by her comments. They could not understand why she would be concerned with "individual" interests.

To add insult to injury, although tax breaks for the rich far outnumber those for the poor, costing society billions each year, it is the poor who are most likely to be targeted for IRS tax audit. Beginning in 1995, the extra money that Congress allowed the IRS to audit the working poor came just as the IRS was cutting back on the resources put into auditing corporations and the rich. In 2002, the IRS audited five of the working poor for every one affluent person (Johnston 2003, 136). Despite the

numerous ways for businesses and the rich to dodge tax payment, it is the working poor who are most closely scrutinized.

How Women Are Particularly Screwed

Women of all races are working outside the home in record
numbers, including married women. Dual-income households
are now the norm. For the first time since capitalism took firm
hold in the United States, black and white women, married and
single, are working outside the home. And women with children
have become full-fledged members of the paid workforce. In
2004, 53 percent of women with children under age three and
73 percent of women with children ages six to seventeen were
in the labor force. Although most women are concentrated in
relatively low-wage, working-class jobs, a growing proportion
now occupy professional-managerial positions. Women now occupy over half of all such positions in the United States (U.S.
Department of Labor 2005). In addition, partly because of their
changing economic status, the number of women seeking economic independence through divorce or remaining single continues to rise. Women at the bottom of the class hierarchy are
increasingly heading families alone, as the job outlook for men,
particularly black men, continues to deteriorate with the shift
from a manufacturing to a service economy.

Yet, as Hartmann and Spalter-Roth argue (1996), public
policy is slow to recognize and reflect these changes, evidenced
in part by the fact that women, as a group, are more likely to
be poor than any other group in the United States. Enduring
gender ideologies that portray women as relatively dependent,
nurturing, and passive, and the home as a place of love and
affection rather than work, productivity, and economic value,
contribute to this persistent phenomenon. Women continue to
be concentrated in jobs and areas of organizations that are characterized as "interactive, expressive, soft," characteristics that
correspond with dominant conceptions of what it means to be

a woman in our society. A significant proportion of working women are employed in low-level service-sector jobs at places like Walmart and MacDonald's where they earn little and are entitled to few, if any, benefits. Women who enter professional-managerial positions are likely to be concentrated in occupations such as teaching or nursing, or areas of organizations that are not seen as directly related to profit and are hence devalued relative to others (that men are more likely to occupy), such as public relations, government relations, and personnel (Scott 1996; Ghiloni 1987).

Moreover, although women continue to be the primary caregivers in the home they are not economically rewarded for the mental, emotional, and financial costs of the work of caregiving. At the same time, the costs associated with motherhood, or parenthood, are astronomical. These costs are not compensated because, unlike other work, caregiving work is not figured into the GNP in this country. Ann Crittenden calls this the "mommy tax" or "caring tax." The mommy tax also includes wages lost when women interrupt their jobs or careers to care for children. Crittenden estimates that the decision to spend her time caring for her child cost her $600,000–$700,000, not counting the loss of a pension. Moreover, women who take a leave from paid work to care for children often find that when they return to the labor force, they do not return to the same jobs. And these costs do not even take into account the value of time, nor do they include the costs associated with the mental, emotional, and physical stress of parenthood (Crittenden 2001). All mothers incur this tax, but for women who are heading households, this tax is often unbearable—and contributes to what sociologists term the "pauperization of motherhood."

Nancy Folbre (2001, 111) argues that children are "public goods" whose future productivity is essential to everybody. Additionally, children will pay taxes and fund social programs, such as social security, from which everyone reaps the benefits.

Crittenden cites the example of the Reed family, consisting of five siblings headed by a single mom. She estimates that these children will probably contribute $3 million in tax revenue and at least $1.5 million to the Social Security Trust Fund. None of this entitles their mother to higher benefits, even though it is because of her provision of care that these children will support the retirement of people who never spent a nickel on a child (Crittenden 2001, 196, 197). Folbre (2001) says that, currently, we think of children like pets, for whom we assume the cost of care and gain personal gratification, but from which we, as a society, get no economic return. She says that when people argue that having a child is a purely personal choice and private obligation, she reminds them that "when their Lab grows up it's not going to pay their social security" (Crittenden 2001, 82).

In addition to the unacknowledged and uncompensated "mommy tax," there are other ways in which the current official tax system reflects and contributes to gender inequality and thus disadvantages women as a group. Once upon a time in this country, prior to the 1940s, individuals were taxed as individuals, even when they were married. Or they could "split" their income, dividing it in half for tax purposes if they wished. Since the 1940s, Congress developed a tax system where family income, not individual income, is taxed at progressive marginal rates. This is based on the assumption that families pool their money, which is not always the case (McCafferty 1997, 24). More significantly, with regard to disadvantaging women, this system reflects a "male bias" in tax policy in the sense that it discourages married women whose husbands earn a higher income from working outside the home. It also contributes to women's poverty because it discourages marriage among poor women. Progressive marginal rates are at the core of these gendered penalties.

As McCafferty (1997, 15) says, "marginal rates help us make decisions." Women's decisions regarding whether or not to work outside the home, who will be the primary caregiver, are related to the tax structure. Since the advent of "modern-style joint filing," the wife's tax bracket depends on her husband's income. As the "secondary earner," the first dollar of her income is taxed at the rate where his has left her; in other words, her income is considered on top of his. Not only does this system encourage families to think in terms of "primary" and "secondary" earners, but also reinforces gender inequality by discouraging women from entering, or remaining in, the paid workforce. McCafferty (1997) provides the example of Earl, who makes $30,000 a year. He pays nothing in tax on the first $20,000, 15 percent on the second $10,000. His wife earns $30,000. Because she is more likely than her husband to file as the secondary earner, her first dollar is taxed at 15 percent. Thus, she pays three times the tax her husband pays. And her $30,000 triggers $4,500 in tax. In most cases, because of persistent gender and family ideologies that assert that men are the breadwinners, women the caretakers of home and family, and because women, on average, earn less than men, it is typically assumed that they are the "secondary" wage earner and therefore are more likely to quit their job. Nada Eissa, economist at the University of California at Berkeley, says of the relationship between taxes and labor force participation, " . . . we think it's strongest for married women" who are usually the family's secondary wage earners and are more likely to consider not working outside the home" (Postrel 2000, 2003).

Poor working women, especially female heads-of-household, are disadvantaged by the current tax system in a different way. In this case, where the "secondary earner" (the man) is hit with a high tax rate on their income, the burden may be more than the family can endure. This helps explain why poor women, among whom African American women make up the greatest share in relation to their proportion of the population, are significantly more likely to be single and stay single. As "primary earners," they simply cannot afford to be married. Or, in the case of married couples, the taxes on the secondary earner are so great that it forces couples to split up.

Because, on average, women earn less than men, assume primary responsibility for the care of children, and pay more taxes in a variety of ways, they generally have less money for savings and investment than men. Gender and class biases embedded in tax and social security policy provide opportunities for those in the dominant groups to accumulate wealth while others are relatively deprived of these opportunities. In 2004, 12.8 percent of all women seventy-five years of age and older were below the poverty line compared with 6.6 percent of men in this age group. Women of color are particularly at high risk for poverty in old age (Hill 2000). Compared with 15.9 percent of black men aged seventy-five and above, 31.5 percent—almost a third—of black women aged seventy-five and older were below the poverty line in 2004 (U.S. Bureau of the Census 2005).

Single mothers are particularly at risk. They generally have less, if any, money to put into savings or retirement plans. Among women who head households, 28 percent of all women and 37 percent of all black women are below the poverty line. Among those with children under eighteen, 43 percent of black women who head households were below the poverty line in 2004. As it is, the amount of money spent by poor women on basic needs is far below the average budgets of single-parent families as a whole (Edin and Lein 1997). As the divorce rate and the proportion of those who never marry increases, the problem of women's poverty will only worsen. All of this comes at a time when those in business and government are pushing for changes in the social security system that will further disadvantage women as a group.

Women make up approximately two-thirds of social security beneficiaries. Half of all older women would be poor if not for the current social security system (Institute for Women's Policy Research 2000). Social security makes up a larger proportion of household income for unmarried women than it did in the 1970s (Williamson and Rix 2000). In the current system, married women receive 50 percent their husband's benefits if they retire at the normal age. If their husband dies, they receive 100 percent of his benefits. If women are divorced, and if they had been married for at least ten years, their benefits are based on their ex-husband's earnings. This system of course does nothing to challenge traditional gender ideologies. As Celeste Colgan, senior fellow with the National Center for Policy Analysis, states, "If she claims benefits through her husband, she gets nothing for all the payroll taxes she's paid . . . Even if she claims on her own work, the net benefit isn't much more than if she'd never worked" (National Center for Policy Analysis [NCPA] 2002). But at least social security, as it is now structured, ensures that women are provided for at some level in old age. Moreover, the current system is "weighted toward low-wage workers who get a larger percentage of preretirement earnings than those who earn higher wages." This works to the advantage of women, who are more likely than men to be concentrated in low-wage jobs. Women are also less likely to occupy jobs where they receive "fat 401(k) plans," so they are especially reliant on social security income (Lieberman 1999).

Proposed changes in the Social Security system, particularly the switch to private retirement accounts, will disproportionately benefit corporations and "unmarried rich men with high incomes who are born well into the next century." Conversely, according to a recent study by the National Committee to Preserve Social Security and Medicare,[1] "the largest group of losers from privatizing Social Security would be women of every income class and marital status" (Lieberman 1999). This is the case for several reasons. First, women have less to invest than men because they earn less, on average, and are more likely to take time off in order to care for children and elderly parents; thus their accounts will yield smaller returns. Second, studies show that women tend to be more conservative than men in their investments, another reason why their accounts are likely to produce smaller yields. Third, because of these factors, a larger share of their accounts would go toward administration (Institute for Women's Policy Research 2000). Administrative costs are estimated at twenty-five to fifty dollars per participant per year (compared with sixteen dollars under the present system) (Hill 2000). Finally, women have a longer life expectancy than men, so their benefits, spread out over the course of their lives, would be lower. As Trudy Lieberman says "privatizing social security won't build much wealth for women, and it will leave elderly women, particularly widows, worse off than they are now" (Lieberman 1999, 6).

WOMEN'S INTERESTS AND BUSINESS HEGEMONY

In the last quarter century, and particularly the last decade, tax and social security policy increasingly reflect and perpetuate economic inequality by providing for the accumulation of money and capital by the upper classes while taking money out of the pockets of those in the lower classes. The tax system not only advances upper-class interests, but also men's interests. If the family wage[2] "cemented the partnership between patriarchy and capital" (Hartmann 1979, 18), then the tax structure keeps adding fresh mortar. Tax policy in the United States is structured in ways that reflect, and perpetuate, women's role not only as "secondary earners," but also as producers of surplus value. Women are primarily responsible for the home and children, work that is essential to the economy but for which they are not paid. Thus, women produce surplus value that mostly serves the interests of men. The current tax regime ensures women's production of surplus value by discouraging women's work outside the home.

There are several reasons why the gendered character of policy in these areas, and its consequences for women's political

and economic interests, is generally overlooked. First, tax and social security policy are not commonly conceptualized as related
to women's issues. Most people do not think about the effects of
progressive marginal rates and other elements of tax and social
security policy on the reproduction of a patriarchal system. This
is partly because we tend not to view state policy, particularly in
the area of revenue collection, as affecting (and affected by) the
interests and identities of the actors involved (Alexander 2000,
60), whether it is women or other groups.

Another contributing factor is that women in the United
States tend to think of themselves as "liberated" and "indepen-
dent," and treated "equally," when in fact they continue to earn a
fraction of what men earn and continue to be responsible for the
lion's share of housework and childcare. Mothers in the United
States experience what Judith Warner calls the "Mommy Mystique." Warner moved to Washington, D.C., from France, with
her three-year-old daughter. The French generally believe that a
person should live a "balanced" life. This is considered especially
true for mothers. A mother whose life includes a satisfying career, romance, and time for herself is considered not only normal, but healthy. A mother who is self-fulfilled is not considered
selfish. This guilt-free image of motherhood stands in sharp contrast to the guilt-ridden version of motherhood in the United
States. Upon her arrival in the United States, Warner's pediatrician told her that she had "better stop trying to have a career."
She found that most of the women she met seemed overridden
with stress, resentment, and exhaustion in their roles as mothers.
They took part-time, "Mommy Track" jobs, or jobs that otherwise "free" them to breastfeed their children for the *right* period
of time, find the *right* pediatrician and dentist, and plan the *right*
birthday party. Warner argues that this increase in hyperparenting "induces stress, anxiety, and depression" in both children and
adults. More shocking to her was that "it didn't seem to dawn
on anyone that there could be another way" (Warner 2005, 15).

It was as if the problem was "so big and so strange that the women could not name it" (Warner 2005, 7).

The Mommy Mystique no doubt contributes to the invisibility of tax policy as a "woman's issue" and vice versa. If the guilt and stress experienced by mothers is seen as normal and natural, and rooted in individual women's endurance or competency, then women are likely to seek individual-level solutions, such as medication,[3] rather than to seek changes at the structural level, such as state policy.

As discussed in the previous chapter, women have recognized, organized around, and struggled for their common interests as women for decades. However, "women's consciousness of their oppression, and the motivation to work to change the system in which they live, is shaped by a complex set of social relations . . . [that are] structured by class, ethnic, and racially specific experiences" (Morgen and Bookman 1988, 11). As Ackelsberg (in Morgen and Bookman 1988, 11) argues, "their particular social locations and multiple responsibilities across [the public and private] realms create distinctive forms of political consciousness and activities." Gilligan (1982) has argued that women and men have "different" moral voices. Women develop an ethic of care, a sense of responsibility and connection to others. But the *character* of women's political activism (how they go about seeking change and *what* they seek to change) is shaped not just by women's collective interests as women; it is also rooted in their common experiences and collective interests as members of particular class, racial, and ethnic groups. Thus, the women with the most visibility and power in the policy arena, those who are in a position to make structural changes that would benefit women as a whole, are women who, because of their race and class locations, are less likely to be compelled to do so.

Although there are women in Washington who lobby for changes in tax and social security policy that serve the interests of ordinary citizens, and women in particular, their numbers are small when compared with the ever-increasing number of women who lobby for corporate interests. In their social locations as white, professional-class women, it is in their best interest to represent those with power and who are seen as credible in the political arena. Groups that represent the interests of women or racial and ethnic minority groups or both "are operating a severe disadvantage in terms of legitimacy. They are lacking the critical resources (e.g. financial means, credibility, contacts and political capital) needed to attain any level of political legitimacy" (Kuersten and Jagemann 2000, 56). Women who lobby for corporate interests are much more likely to be taken seriously and listened to by those in government than those who lobby for women's interests. And because the interests they represent are viewed as credible and legitimate by society as a whole, and by government officials in particular, they are likely to reap higher material rewards for their work than those who represent "women's" groups.

Corporations exert unequalled and unquestioned power in the United States through their hegemonic control over the economy and people's lives. If we were to consider only those decisions that business makes on a routine basis, "excluding anything that would generally be considered ethically or legally dubious or that a significant fraction of elected officials disputes as business's right . . . exclude any actions that are done only through business's influence on government," we see that business has enormous power and control over peoples' lives. Corporations make decisions about where people work, the hours they work, when they get to rest, who works, and who doesn't. Corporations decide what we buy, how much, and the quality of our purchases. They make decisions about the very air people breathe—in and out of the workplace. Corporations are granted the right to make all these, and many more, decisions about the way we live. "If the government fails to act, big business can do what it wishes" (Clawson, et al. 1992, 183, 185).

The extent and nature of business power in the United States remains largely invisible and unquestioned because of something Antonio Gramsci (1972) called "hegemony." Hegemony, for Gramsci, is a "culture and set of institutions that structure life patterns and coerce a particular way of life" (Clawson, et al. 1992, 23). Much like racism in the South prior to the 1960s, the economic power of business is incorporated in a set of social structures and practices that are accepted, not only by business but also by the mass. Business's economic power is seen as normal and natural. Because of this, most of business's influence in government is centered on *preventing* legislation that would interfere with "business as usual"—persuading government officials *not* to take action on legislation that would hurt them. At the same time, it must be acknowledged that business power is not uncontested in the political realm. One has only to remember the case of the Pinto, a car produced by Ford during the 1960s that burst into flames when hit from behind because of a faulty gas tank. Ford knew that there was a problem and yet continued with production of the Pinto. Although high-paid corporate lobbyists and lawyers were successful at delaying regulations that would have required Ford to fix the Pinto much sooner, consumer activists (led by Ralph Nader)[4] brought enough public attention to the issue (and victims filed enough law suits) that Ford was eventually forced to make changes.

Because business power is unequalled but not uncontested, corporations must be constantly vigilant in the political realm. Political action committee (PAC) contributions are one tool that corporations use to ensure an "ear" in government when an issue arises. And corporations have the potential to raise as much money for their PAC as they want because of their ability to coerce contributors in a way that no other kind of PAC can. All an executive needs to say to an employee is "this is important to the company, and I hope you can support me on this." This "loose indicator" of being part of the "team" sends a clear message that, if you don't contribute to the PAC, you better not count on that next raise. Thus, unlike other organizations, corporations have the potential to raise unlimited amounts of PAC money (Clawson et al. 1992). Although current contribution limits prevent any one corporation from contributing enormous amounts of money to particular candidates, when business unites in its political activity, and it does,[5] the effects are significant. When President Clinton's budget plan for 2000 proposed stiff penalties to rein in corporate tax shelters, Kenneth Kies, managing partner at PricewaterhouseCoopers, got on the phone to his friends in the business community. Kies recruited fifteen corporations to pay $10,000 apiece in order to gain access to key lawmakers to make the case that the provisions were "a wholesale assault on the corporate tax departments of our clients." Kies also enlisted approximately twenty companies in a "'Leasing Coalition' to fight an Administration proposal to curb a specific corporate tax shelter" (Stone 1999, 944).

PAC contributions are only one tool that corporations have at their disposal in times of need. Overlapping career paths also ensure a special connection between business and government. Kenneth Kies, the corporate official at PricewaterhouseCoopers, is a former chief of staff on the Joint Committee on Taxation and former Republican tax counsel on the House Ways and Means Committee (Stone 1999). Bush's choice for secretary of the Treasury, John Snow, spent twenty years as CEO of CSX Corporation, a major tax dodger. In three of four years, from 1999 to 2001, CSX paid no federal income tax at all (Citizens for Tax Justice 2002).

In addition to campaign contributions and overlapping career paths, business also has abundant resources to wine and dine government officials, and invite them to private, secluded

receptions and retreats where together they eat, drink, soak
in spas, play golf, and discuss public policy to the exclusion
of everyone else. Leaders of organizations such as the Secure
Retirement Coalition, a business policy discussion group that
advocates for private accounts, speak at these gatherings where
they (re)frame social security as a "market issue." New social
security markets, they say, are springing up—single women,
working women, widowed or divorced women with hefty in-
heritances. And corporations, particularly financial institutions,
have a "vested interest" in these markets. While they soak in
the spa or share a glass of wine with government officials, they
do not discuss the fact that, among those who work outside
the home, women are more likely to be poor than any other
group. Nor do they mention that this is particularly the case for
women who are single heads of household. And they do not
bring up the fact that half of older women would be poor if
not for the current social security system. Other alternatives to
the present system, such as using corporate taxes to fund social
security, are denounced or immediately dismissed.

Business's hegemonic power and control over the economy
and people's everyday lives ensures corporate lobbyists a legitimacy and credibility in the political realm. In many ways this
makes their jobs easier, and more rewarding, than those of other
lobbyists or activists in Washington. Because they are more likely
to be viewed as credible and legitimate, corporate lobbyists are
better positioned to develop strong and enduring formal and
informal ties with those in government. As a result, they are also
more likely to gain access to legislators and their staffs on key
issues and information about what is happening in government.
Thus they are better positioned than others to exert influence in
the legislative realm. For white professional-class women, corporate government relations jobs provide visibility, economic
security, and political power that they would not have were they
to represent women's interests (or other non-business interests).

Conflict of Interest?

Women's involvement in corporate lobbying is significant for maintaining and strengthening business-government ties, thus contributing to business power in the political realm. My research finds that women corporate lobbyists are as active as their male colleagues in networking with people in government, although there are significant differences in the character of their networking activity. Women are less likely than their male colleague to socialize with legislators, but more likely to socialize with legislative staff, particularly women staffers (Scott 1996). Although researchers argue that women's networks with other women provide "health" benefits (Smith-Lovin and McPherson 1993), or psychological "satisfaction" (Martin 1993a), most argue that women are better off establishing "instrumental" ties with those in top policy-making positions (who are mostly men). In the case of women corporate lobbyists, an alternative perspective (Scott 1996) is that ties with women staffers are as important, if not more important, in shaping legislation as are ties with legislators. Corporate lobbyists and legislative staffers made this point repeatedly: "It could be a vote, though in general the votes, you've either got them or you don't. They can become inconsequential. You get a few where it's real tight. But you don't see that many one-vote decisions in these bodies. It comes down to staff work, when they are writing the bills, whether they will include your views in their thought process, whether you can get in the door to see them. That's a big one."

Moreover, in response to their exclusion from old boys networks, women corporate lobbyists are forming their own, "girls" networks, as one corporate lobbyist put it, and policy discussion organizations to share information and form relationships with other women lobbyists and women in government. The Tax Alliance, for example, holds regular meetings in Washington and annual retreats. Invited speakers include women (often past members of the organization) who serve as advisors to key tax-writing committees in government (such as the House Ways and Means and the Senate Finance Committees) and Treasury Department officials and staff. Discussed in greater depth in the following chapters, women in business and government do and use gender (both masculinity and femininity) within these organizational contexts in ways that help strengthen their relationships and thus contribute to their own career advancement and business's influence in the political sphere.

Nancy Folbre says that individuals are in "contradictory positions," and as such they "often join coalitions that are inimical to some of their interests" (Folbre 1993, 330). As corporate lobbyists, women act in ways that are often contradictory to their positions, and interests, as women. It could be argued that we should not expect women lobbyists, or other professional women, to be responsible for women's interests. Hanchard makes this case for black professionals. "Never in the history of capitalism have the middle and upper classes been expected to assist in the socioeconomic advancement of working-class people, yet this is the common assumption among many U.S. citizens about the roles that middle-class blacks (this includes black public intellectuals) are to play . . .". He further argues that black middle-class professionals have had to "provide defenses for their personal successes amid high black unemployment, urban violence, and whatever else has been deemed to be a 'black problem.'" (Hanchard 1996, 104) Hanchard argues that it is "ridiculous" to expect black public intellectuals, and other black professionals, to always make their work relevant to the social problems of the black community. Likewise, we could argue that it is ridiculous to expect that professional women make their work relevant to "women's issues."

To the contrary, others argue that black professionals are essentially "selling out"—they are succeeding and profiting at the expense the black working-class community. Adolph

Reed's 1995 article in the *Village Voice* sparked a renewed and intense debate over the "accountability" of black professionals, particularly "public intellectuals." Reed and others argue that many black public intellectuals are "sadly disconnected from the social forces and struggles of the working class and poor people's communities" (Marable 1995, 35). Moreover, Reed is critical of the inattention of black elites to the "absence of sustained investigation of institutional forms of power . . ." Blacks should be "fighting against ratification of the balanced budget amendment, crafting responses to the so-called tort reform, and finding ways to counter the assault on the Bill of Rights" (Hanchard 1996, 102).

For all the debate surrounding black capitalists' abandonment of the "black community" and "black problems," business continues to view black professionals as representative of their race and of racial interests. Zweigenhaft and Domhoff (2001, 273) find, for example, that most blacks "have not risen through the executive ranks on the companies on whose boards they sit, but have been chosen for certain expertise or in some cases to provide what [they] call 'buffers, ambassadors and tokens.'" Collins (1997) likewise argues that African Americans are segregated into "racialized" positions within organizations, such as human relations and affirmative action officers, positions that are relatively devalued and thus more vulnerable than others when downsizing occurs.

Although women continue to be segregated into jobs and areas of organization that are feminized, such as public relations and government relations, they are increasingly less restricted to working on women's issues. In the case of women corporate lobbyists, not only are they increasingly entering policy areas once viewed as male, but areas where their work leads to policy outcomes that actually counter women's interests. While the debate rages concerning black professionals' accountability to the interests of the black community, we do not see the same attention to women professionals' accountability to women as a group. Women increasingly struggle for interests that compete with, and in many ways work against, the interests of women as a whole, and yet this is not problematized or even recognized as an issue by social scientists or political pundits.

One possible explanation is that gender inequality, and the social forces that perpetuate it, are much more likely to be overlooked or dismissed than other forms of inequality in the United States. From very early on, children are identified and separated by gender without question or challenge. Teachers in elementary school start the day by greeting the class with "Hello, boys and girls." Lines are formed at recess according to gender (Thorne 1993). Just imagine teachers welcoming students by saying, "Hello, blacks and whites," or forming lines on the playground by race: "All the blacks line up over here, all the whites over there." You can bet there would be an immediate revolt and public outcry. Examples of overt sexism are everywhere, and are relatively unchallenged and even unnoticed, in our society. We are constantly surrounded by images of men as relatively powerful and strong, women as relatively passive and weak—from women with spike heels in submissive (if not fatal) poses on the front pages of magazines to women being paraded around on leashes, as was the case during a recent MTV Video Music Awards show. During the show, popular rapper Snoop Dogg proceeded to prance around the stage with two black women in S&M garb on dog leashes. He was not yanked off the stage. He was not captured and arrested. He was applauded! Not only did he get away with performing this act, many companies would have loved to see their logo printed on the leashes. Can anyone imagine a white man parading around with two black men on dog leashes and getting away with it, much less profiting from the act? And yet we tend to think of the problem of gender equality as practically wiped out in the United States. Thus, when women in the workplace come together to act in ways that conflict with women's interests as a whole, they are less likely to be viewed as doing anything questionable, dubious, or harmful.

Perhaps more importantly, race and class interact much differently than do gender and class in our society. Because of a different history of oppression and hardship as a group, and the continued relationship between race and economic disadvantage in the United States, African Americans as a group are more acutely aware of the political necessity for racial and ethnic consciousness and unity. Historically, women's social class status has been determined primarily by their husbands' class position. Thus, white women have always been in contradictory positions with regard to joining coalitions inimical to their interests. When African Americans form coalitions to act in ways that serve to disadvantage the interests of the entire group, they are likely to be seen as "traitors." When women form all-women coalitions to struggle for corporate interests that result in disadvantaging women as a group, they are not seen as acting in ways antithetical to women's interests.

The following chapter looks closely at the Tax Alliance, a policy discussion group composed of women in business and government who are experts in the area of tax policy. Using the Tax Alliance as a case study, we will explore how women, through their organizational connections and activities, and by doing and using gender in organizational contexts, strengthen business-government relations and business power.

CHAPTER 4

Warm Springs and Hot Topics at the Tax Alliance Retreat

DOING GENDER AND
DOING BUSINESS

IMAGINE YOU ARE enveloped in a warm wrap of linens that have been steamed in a fragrant blend of natural herbs. You then receive a hydroptimale treatment to prevent dehydrated skin. Next you receive a special treatment to increase the consumption of oxygen by the skin, resulting in an even, fresh, and luminous complexion. You take a leisurely soak in a luxurious mineral bath, warm water cascading around you, leaving you in a state of total relaxation and enchantment. Your skin is rubbed with raspberry oil, wrapped, and allowed to re-moisturize itself. You are member of the Tax Alliance, a women-only organization whose members are representatives of the top tiers of business and government and who get together once a year at a luxury hotel and spa to soak in mineral baths, enjoy facials and body wraps, bowl, play golf, dine on the finest food—and discuss the hottest tax, social security, and health care policy issues of the day.

It has been several decades since Domhoff presented his eye-opening analysis of the Bohemian Grove, where social bonds between the captains of industry and high-level politicians, who are mostly men, are solidified and policy cohesion enhanced through informal discussion, activities, rituals, and ceremonies (Domhoff 1974). Because policy organization research has focused mostly on the networks of those who occupy the top tiers of business and government, many specialized policy discussion groups (where women have entered as more than just tokens) have been overlooked. This chapter examines the significance of a women-only policy discussion group, the Tax Alliance (pseudonym), and its annual retreat, for solidifying the business-government relationship. In addition, building on the work of others (Martin and Collinson 1999; Martin 1996, 2001, 2003; Moore 1987, 1988), it examines how gender is produced and used within the context of the Tax Alliance retreat and the potential consequences for business-government relations.

The Tax Alliance

The Tax Alliance was founded in the mid-1980s by a group of women from the corporate sector in their attempt to combat various forms of gender discrimination. Some women who represented top corporations in Washington began to realize that they were being treated like second-class citizens in terms of prestige and promotion: "It was like we were still serving coffee," says one of the founders. They also began to realize that they were being left out of the arenas where important policy discussions took place and where there were opportunities to network with key people in government. Several of the original members of the Tax Alliance explained that the final straw was when a woman corporate-government relations official was "kicked out" of a Washington power breakfast. That night the Tax Alliance was born. As one of the founders, a corporate-government relations vice president, said, "A couple of my girlfriends and I got on my Rolodex one night and started our own girls' network." Thus it all began with a small group of women who decided to form their own tax group in order to provide each other with career support and exchange important policy information. From its inception, the Tax Alliance included not only corporate friends, but also friends who worked on the Hill.

Today the Tax Alliance remains a small, exclusive group of women who represent business and government. The criteria for corporate membership are strict, limited to women who spend at least 90 percent of their time working on tax issues and who are sponsored by other Tax Alliance women. For the women in government who specialize in this areas, becoming a member is a "piece of cake":

> For the private sector it is very big. Like you are put on a list, the waiting list, and then when someone leaves you get to come in, and so it is a pretty hard and fast number. It is a big deal when you get admitted because now you are in the Tax Alliance. I think for the public sector folks, it is more of like you didn't have to work to get in. I mean if you are on the Way and Means, Finance, or Joint Tax you are automatically admitted. So it is no big deal really to get in but for the private sector it is. You know, it took me one day to join the group. It was no big deal because I am one of the people that all these private lobbyists are trying to get to know. (legislative aide, member of Congress)

Groups with "strict membership criteria," where there are a "chosen few," are more likely to be cohesive (Domhoff 2001, 45). The Tax Alliance could be described as a cohesive group, and what makes them so is not only a matter of size or selection criteria but also the settings in which they interact.

The Tax Alliance holds monthly meetings in Washington, D.C., where legislative staff and government officials speak to the group on a variety of tax-related topics. While the monthly meetings provide useful information about what business and government are planning, the annual retreat of the Tax Alliance is where business and government not only exchange key bits of information, but also establish close bonds. Every year the

Tax Alliance retreat is held at a hotel and spa that is, at other times, host to other Washington policy groups as well as scores of prominent people and famous politicians. The site provides a relaxed and luxurious environment and an ideal "off-the-record" atmosphere where no reporters or other "outsiders" are allowed. What better place to facilitate cohesiveness among business and government representatives than a retreat that takes place in a resort and spa setting where one is treated to skin therapies such as the "Cascades," the "ultimate in relaxation, rejuvenation and attention .... designed to make you feel very special .... You can expect to indulge your senses and relax in nothing less than the most luxurious surroundings" (from the hotel brochure).

In the year that I conducted my research, sixty-two Tax Alliance women came together in this relaxed and luxurious setting. In attendance were five counsels and public liaisons to the U.S. Treasury, three high-level advisors to key governmental tax and finance committees, eight congressional staffers representing members who sit on tax-writing committees, twenty corporate-government relations officials, and nine business-related trade association representatives. The remainder were lawyers and consultants representing over thirty-six major U.S. companies. The title of this particular year's retreat was "Moving Toward the Millennium—Show Me the Money."

THE PRIVATE-PUBLIC
(AKA BUSINESS-GOVERNMENT) PARTNERSHIP

There are at least a half-dozen Washington tax groups financed by labor, citizens, and other groups, but when asked whether government representatives soak in hot tubs with representatives of other tax groups, the answer from the Tax Alliance women is unanimously and unabashedly "of course not:" "There is a National Taxpayers Union. There are other organizations that I think you can be part of just because you are a citizen, but I don't know of another organization that asks the public sector to become members. In fact my sense is that they don't, I mean they tend not to exist or not to be very powerful, but maybe they are in terms of their lobbying" (legislative aide, member of Congress). Major corporations can (and do) draw from their enormous treasuries to fund extravagant events where government officials are present and cover the cost of their membership and meeting attendance.

More importantly, policy makers and their staffs do not see a need to attend retreats with representatives of citizens groups or other organizations because they do not view tax and social security issues as "public" issues. Social scientists have long shown that big business and government enjoy a privileged and exclusive relationship though the highly interlocked structure of political and economic decision making in the United States. Listening to the women of the Tax Alliance describe their relationships, it is clear that this special and exclusive "partnership" is taken for granted. One legislative aide makes this point clearly when she says, "It is very much a partnership. You know the private and public sectors are working in tax policy and need each other basically." Interviewees refer to government and corporate officials as part of a tax "club," "community," or "family."[1] Another legislative aids remarks, "I knew pretty much about the group when I came to the first luncheon. I saw some fantastic people that were involved with it and recognized it as an opportunity to learn. It is an opportunity to know all the people who are going to be in the tax community. The tax community becomes very much a large family after a while." Apparently citizens, labor, and environmental groups are not part of the tax "family."

One corporate-government official refers to the Tax Alliance as "sort of the vehicle for the creation of a sense of community." This sense of community is continuously constructed and reconstructed at the retreat and in Washington through a dominant ideology that is reinforced through language, gestures,

symbols, and activities. Government representatives are not considered guests, but rather members of the organization. Upon
check-in at the retreat, all participants are given identification
tags with names only, which suggests that organizational affili-
ation is insignificant or unimportant. They all receive the same
ten-pound binder containing the program, list of participants,
speaker bios, and various other literature concerning the hot issues to be considered and discussed at the retreat. Both government and corporate representatives are listed on the program as
organizational leaders, committee members, and speakers.[2] All
of this reinforces a dominant ideology that asserts that business
and government representatives are part of the same big family. According to several of the women, it also provides a way
for corporations to get around the gift ban: "The way it works,
given our current Ethics rule situation and gift ban prohibitions
and all that kind of stuff, is that they are active participants in
the program and retreat. Everyone has to take an active role,
a substantive role in speaking panels, discussions on the issues
that are relevant to their professional activities in the House or
Senate or Treasury Department" (corporate-government relations representative).

This ideology is also reinforced though rituals that take place
at the retreat and in Washington. There is the annual Christmas
Party, for example, where the public- and private-sector members of the Tax Alliance write, direct, and act in skits. Key government officials are often the subjects of, and sometimes take
part in, the skits and musical numbers. One corporate representative who founded the Tax Alliance describes the event as the
"hottest ticket in Washington":

> I think the nicest compliment I had is when I invited this
> year some of my colleagues from New York, and they were
> saying, here are all the people that they read about in the
> *New York Times* and *Wall Street Journal* up there dancing in

goofy costumes. Here is [the] IRS Commissioner, and you know he didn't even know what was up when we wrote a song to him, and, you know, he was just blown away. So the Tax Alliance sort of affirms and defines the community that most of the other organizations simply don't do. (corporate-government relations representative)

Similarly, there is a ritual that takes place on the final evening of the retreat called the "Sequins Only Banquet and Award Ceremony." The award ceremony begins in a way not unlike one of the rituals that takes place at the Bohemian Grove retreat, where the High Priest lights the fire at the "Lamb of Fellowship" (Domhoff 1974). The award ceremony opens with the official "Prize Queen," a round woman with graying hair who is one of the group's founders, bouncing onto and across a stage wearing a glittery tiara on her head and carrying pom poms in each hand (cheerleader-style). She proceeds to dance around on the stage on her tiptoes, turning around and around, eliciting howls of laughter from the audience. After a few introductory remarks, she turns the show over to a public-sector woman (a Senate Finance Committee advisor) who first presents bowling awards for "best bumper bowler," "bowler with the most strikes," and "best bowling outfit." She then presents phallic-shaped golf trophies (backscratchers made of wooden sticks in the shape of clubs with balls on each side) to several participants. The audience roars with laughter; a woman at my table comments that her "cheeks hurt" from laughing so hard. After the bowling and golf awards, the Prize Queen selects two women from the audience to serve as her "Fairly Good Godmothers." One represents a corporate lobbying firm in Washington and the other is an advisor to a government tax-writing committee. While the official duty of the Fairly Good Godmother is to hand out miscellaneous prizes, an unofficial and unspoken responsibility is to make funny remarks while doing so. Many of the prizes have sexual overtones, such as lingerie. Throughout the ceremony, the women in the audience clearly seem to share an understanding and appreciation of the jokes.

Rituals like the annual Christmas Party and the Sequins Only banquet that bring private and public representatives together as active participants—joking, laughing, dancing, wearing "goofy costumes"—work as a glue that bonds business and government representatives. Active involvement and participation in these rituals and ceremonies creates a vested interest in the organization and its goal, pressures participants toward conformity, and reinforces the ideology of togetherness. The added sexual component of these rituals further serves to solidify the relationship. As Domhoff suggests in the *Bohemian Grove,* sharing a "Bulls' Balls Lunch" is likely to contribute to a sense of brotherhood among the participants (Domhoff 1974, 21). Although they do not go as far as to import a "large supply of testicles from a newly castrated herd," as do the Bohemians, the Tax Alliance women create a sisterhood through the use of sex and sexuality in their rituals and ceremonies.

The business-government partnership is reinforced ideologically through language, symbols, and rituals in Washington and at the retreat, but there is also a codependency relationship built into the structure of their careers. Women who are legislative aides, or who serve in some other advisory capacity within government, look to the business sector for job mobility and advancement. According to a longtime member, when the Tax Alliance began, "a lot of the women had been teachers" before landing jobs as corporate-government relations officials. These days the most common trajectory begins with a law or public policy degree from a prestigious institution, ideally in combination with experience on the Hill as staff or counsel to a key committee. After working in the public sector for a short time, the women typically move on to jobs in the private sector. As one top Senate aide said, "There aren't many women my age (mid-forties) still working on the Hill." Contacts made at the Tax Alliance retreat provide the public sector women with a "building block career-wise." The networking opportunities that abound at the retreat provide the public-sector women with opportunities to get to know, learn from, and bond with private sector women: "Hill staffers are generally so much younger than lobbyists. I mean these people have been around so much and they have to come in and teach me, who doesn't know anything, and they have been through twenty tax bills in their lives. You know this is the first time I've come this close to a tax bill that I have worked on, and I had to come [to the retreat] and talk with these women. You know, they are willing to come talk to me about the issue and teach me from scratch. They have much more experience than Hill staffers" (legislative aide, member of Congress).

Teaching and Learning
(aka Information and Access)

The Tax Alliance women do not hide or defend the special and exclusive partnership business and government enjoy around tax-related issues. They resist, however, being referred to as a "policy" or "lobbying" organization. Participants use terms such as "educational" to describe the organization and their relationships. They distinguish themselves from the Tax Council and other policy organizations in Washington. According to one legislative aide, "The Tax Council (a mixed-gender organization) I think will occasionally submit testimony on a hearing. The Tax Alliance would never do that. We aren't about taking policy stands. It is more to educate on specific issues." Likewise, a corporate lobbyist reports, "It [the Tax Alliance] is to promote communication, education on substantive tax issues between public and private sector members. I mean it is very helpful for the public sector and it is very, very helpful to the private sector members and it is sort of . . . . we help each other around education issues."

The communication and education aspects of the retreat are in fact *very, very* helpful for the private-sector members in the sense that they provide corporate representatives with a heads up on what government is doing and planning, often before policy issues are made public. Domhoff (1974, 15) describes how the Lakeside Talks given at the Bohemian Grove by politicians provide business and government officials present with a "good feel for how a particular problem will be handled." Likewise, formal sessions and informal discussions that take place at the Tax Alliance retreat provide participants with a good feel for how the government is going to handle certain tax-related issues. Each day key government representatives give speeches in which they outline their plans. For example, on the first day of the retreat a chief counsel to an important government tax-writing committee gave a speech entitled "Perspectives on Where We Have Been and Where We Are Going." The following day, a woman who is staff director for a government policy committee gave a talk entitled, "A Review of the Budget Rules of the House and Senate and Their Impact on Tax Legislation." Later in the morning, two Treasury Department representatives and a woman who is chief counsel to a government finance committee spoke on "A Dialogue Between Public and Private Sector Representatives on the Highlights and Lowlights of the Administration's Budget and Other Tax Agenda Items." Throughout the retreat, legislative aides and other government representatives presented speeches on tax, health and Medicare reform, and social security policy issues. As one corporate official says, it is about bringing people together to form relationships and to "educate them about issues that may be important or are becoming important."

On the second day of the retreat a past member of the Tax Alliance who now occupies a high-level staff position within the Treasury presented a speech concerning tax shelters at a corporate-sponsored luncheon. After some relatively brief and general remarks concerning tax shelters and social security, she announced that some "white papers" would be coming out from the Treasury "sometime this summer." Here is how one corporate representative describes a Treasury white paper:

> It is a policy paper more than anything else. These are the general policies we want to lay out. It lays out their position and what they intend to do in the future with it, and so a white paper is more of a treaties kind of thing. People wait for the Treasury white papers on specific things. Right now they are waiting for the white paper on tax shelters because it will outline very specifically what some of the definitions are that they are talking about—like what is the definition of a tax shelter. So, the white paper is, you know, sort of what their starting point is for their position—sort of a treaties of the Treasury's opinion on things, but it is not a specific rule that says you must follow this.

A white paper is a statement of the Treasury's understanding and interpretation of certain policy issues, which, according to the same corporate government relations official, may or may not "include some recommendations on how they think that the problem as they see it should get fixed." The white paper is discussed and debated among the relevant parties, who are given a chance to respond before it is drafted into a bill or regulation. "Anyone who could possibly be affected by the policy and what may come out of it will want to see it," one legislative aide told me. Because of how the public policy "community" is conceived of, "anyone possibly affected" in effect means business and government representatives. As one corporate woman said: "Copies will be delivered to Congress and, once it is released, it will be faxed all over town to all the private sector folks. The white paper is supposed to give the policy community broadly, meaning the private and public sectors, an idea of where the Treasury is going before they actually draft a regulation or draft a bill that they are going to send to Capitol Hill." At the retreat, the Tax Alliance women (and particularly the "private sector folks") "anxiously await" information from their Treasury official buddy about when the white papers will be released and a preview (or at least a hint) of what they will contain. Because of the close friendships and mutual understandings they have developed over time as a result of their overlapping careers and shared history, there is little need for the speaker to be explicit in her communication with the women in the audience. She began her career working for a legislator who was on the House Ways and Means, then worked for a Washington law firm as a tax lobbyist, and now occupies a high-level advisory position within the Treasury.[3] Thus, she can effectively make use of jokes, facial expressions, and gestures to convey information:

> Everybody knows where she is from, they know where she started in this whole thing, and what she used to work on when she lobbied and what her positions were because she was in the private sector and now she is on the Hill. She has been with the Tax Alliance probably since its onset, and so there are a lot of close friendships that have been there forever, and, as she has moved into her various positions, people know her background. They know her feelings about things, they know her political bents, and so there are a lot of probably inside jokes that happen just because of knowing someone well and feeling comfortable with them. It was like having one of your own come and talk to you, but now they have moved way up. It is like if you had a colleague that you worked with on a daily basis all of a sudden become President of the University coming back and saying here is how we are going to do things. You know that you know the inside track on their feelings . . . . (corporate-government relations official)

At the end of her speech she assured the audience that the Treasury plan will go through a "thorough evaluation and study," and that it will be open to "all outside sources" and "everyone will have a chance to provide input," which elicited subdued chuckles from the audience. She then added quickly, "Nothing is being kept secret."

Perhaps even more important than acquiring a "heads up" is the special access women gain through the bonds that are created and reinforced at the Tax Alliance retreat. Formal presentations provide useful information and insights on a broad level, but the friendships formed between the women ensure them and their corporations privileged access to the legislative process when a particular concern arises. As one corporate official says concerning the Treasury official's speech:

> While it is not open to the press, she is making a public statement, so it is not like she is speaking secretly with her best buddy. Even though she is friendly with everyone in the room, she cannot give us real, real, real inside information . . . . But you may have a better chance of getting to her. She may return your phone call, she may have a meeting with you because you are a member of the group that she may not necessarily have with someone else. So, it gives you access in a way that you probably wouldn't have . . . . It really is access more than anything else. It is the same with the staff on the Hill. When you go to talk with them, they are more likely to return your phone call.

Friendships made at the Tax Alliance retreat and other informal activities provide a foot in the door:

> My schedule is insane. I mean it is packed every day, and in this town people get what I call "bug time" which is okay. The relationship is far more important because I will call them, you know, I have time to call them back. I know your issues, why don't you come on in, two minutes, and you know we can be out the door. So, you know that

relationships I have in the Tax Alliance sort of precipitate some of my business relationships here because then they can say, well I saw you, or you know they will get to me right on the fly when I come in the door. Do you have two minutes if I come into your office and talk to you? (legislative aide, Senator)

And when there is a prior and personal relationship, most times all it takes is about two minutes.

Friendships made at the retreat are also helpful to legislative staff should a question arise regarding an issue of concern to business: "Everyone kept telling me, you've got to join this group and the contacts that you make will help you career-wise, and you just get a basic knowledge. And it is true because some people that I met—I never met them before—but I felt very comfortable calling them saying, you know, you were at that retreat and, by the way, here is an issue that I know your company has talked about. Will you explain it to me or can you—and so contact-wise it helped a lot" (legislative aide, member of Congress). Private meetings and phone calls are not necessarily arranged for the purpose of doing business. Because of their busy schedules, legislative aides often meet with their friends in the private sector for breakfast or lunch in informal and relaxed settings like that of the retreat:

The private sector inter-linkage .... Maybe it is just because I feel the caliber of the private sector participants in this group is very good, it is very high and frequently they are a step ahead on what the next issue of the day is going to be because they have been sitting around organizing it and talking about, before they hit the Hill and start lobbying it. And so by talking to them, I can frequently find out what the next issue is that I am going to get lobbied on by a bunch of people. So, I can actually keep a little bit ahead of the curve. Now, they will try to find out from me what the response is going to be and how the staff is reacting, so there is information I can give back. But frequently they can give me a heads up on what is coming, the next wave of things that are coming and some of the politics of who is behind what, who is talking to who, what organizations are banding behind doing things, which groups are opposing, who is paying for what. I mean that still is easier to get by talking to the private sector people, in particular on an informal basis. It is a lot easier to get it when you are sitting around and talking at lunch. (legislative aide, Senator)

As noted earlier, the Tax Alliance is not a policy organization in the same sense as the mixed-gender Tax Council. It does not issue formal, unified statements or position papers. As compared with the Tax Council, it is " .... not a group that puts out responses to tax policies, like the President's budget." However, Tax Alliance members are privy to information about policy plans before they become public and are given opportunities to respond. Moreover, through the close friendships and mutual understandings, they are unusually advantaged in their ability to "read between the lines" to gain privileged information and access that is crucial to influencing policy.[4] Informal and out-of-the-way settings like that of the Tax Alliance retreat provide an ideal environment for business and government to "work together" on policy issues to the exclusion of others.

THE SIGNIFICANCE OF GENDER

The women of the Tax Alliance work hard to present a particular image of their organization, relationships, and goings-on at the retreat. The group was originally called the Women's Tax Alliance, but very soon after its inception the name was changed to omit "Women." Both the corporate lobbyists and legislative aides at the retreat indicated that they are sensitive (some downright opposed) to being "pigeon-holed as a bunch of girls who really want to be pigeon-holed as a bunch of tax professionals," a group of women who are more interested in the "women's side of things" than the more "important" tax side of things. Says a corporate government affairs official, "The Tax Alliance is much more of a professional group. We talk about tax issues, we talk about much more technical stuff, and it is more based on what is happening legislatively or what's going on right now. It is not about—it is about the tax side of things, not the women's side of things." A legislative aide echoes these sentiments: "I think that's why it has broken the mold in a way. They don't identify themselves as a women's group. It is a credible group in town and maybe it is because they don't push that. I didn't feel at the retreat that it was a big women's rights type of thing at all. We didn't deal with women's issues. We dealt with tax issues that were very important, and I think that's what helps make it more credible in a way—just trying to break away from that."

The reluctance by Tax Alliance members to be seen as "just" a women's social group and the emphasis placed on the "very important" technical, issues-oriented nature of the meetings are at least in part an attempt to counter characterizations of their group as expressive, soft, more interested in talk than task—traditionally female characterizations (Kanter 1977). One corporate woman explains how, upon returning from the retreat, she reassured her boss that the meeting provided "substantive" information and was not just some kind of "male-bashing event":

My chief of staff is very interested because he was skeptical at first, you know, just because he was like, what kind of group is this? He wasn't sure how credible the group really was but I showed him. I told him who was there, and he wanted to know just sort of—you know, what do they talk about all weekend? Was it just some male-bashing event all weekend long? I told him it wasn't—it was substantive. So, the only thing he would want to know is if I had some good substantive information that I found out at the meeting. I said [a key member of the House Ways and Means] spoke to the group and told us something worthwhile. (legislative aide, member of Congress)

The Tax Alliance women structure the retreat in ways that emphasize their engagement in substantive activity, "real" work. The ten-pound binder and numerous other materials, the formal sessions and speeches scheduled each day from 8:30 a.m. to noon, and the formal luncheons, are considered by the leaders of the organization as necessary to put forth the "correct" image.

The Tax Alliance women work hard to characterize themselves, their organization, and the retreat in traditionally masculine ways, as substantive, instrumental, technical. At the same time, they describe their group as "different" than men's organizations and "special." When asked whether they want to remain an all-woman organization, all but one of the women answered affirmatively. When asked why, most remark that they do not want the organization and its retreat to lose their special character or charm. "I don't know," says a corporate-government relations official. "Maybe it is a transitional issue [whether to admit men], but this issue we have debated for, I don't know, probably fifteen years, and what it comes to is that they [the members] really don't want to lose whatever that special charm is." When encouraged to articulate what makes the organization so special, the women say things like "people are more comfortable in an all-women's group" and "having a woman that you are talking to is generally easier to do." According to the legislative aide to a Senator:

It seems as though there aren't that many of what I consider to be, you know, ball-breaking hard women that are members. Maybe tax just doesn't lend itself to it, but I don't think so. They don't seem to have those tendencies on display as

part of that group, and maybe it is because they don't have
to. They are in a women-only group. They don't have to
be out there competing with men. They don't have to be
the cut-throat sort of—and so you do get a sense that there
is more trust and more ability to have a conversation because, even to the extent that you might have those kinds of
women in the group, they are not as likely to take out their
knives when they are dealing with other women in that
particular group than they might otherwise. So maybe that's
what the sense of security comes from.

The Tax Alliance women view the retreat environment and the
organization as non-threatening, non-competitive, safe, and secure,
and this seems to breed a certain level of trust among them.

Even though they are competing for limited jobs and information, and most are very vocal and assertive women, highly
expert in tax-related policy areas, most say that they have found
a "safe haven." According to one government relations official,
"We have got an awful lot of assertive women in this group, and
it is nice to feel at home. Psychologically I think it is safer. You
are willing to take the risk. People are there to help you. There
is not the fear that there is going to be some high-powered
woman—but it is not as though the women are necessarily weak
either you know."

Retreat activities are also viewed as non-competitive and
"softened." Things would be different, says a corporate official,
if men were to become members: "I think it would change the
whole sort of feel of our retreat to have men as members because,
you know, this group has picked places that appeal to a lot of
what the women want out of a business pleasure retreat which is
the spa facilities, as opposed to 'Let's have a ....' But I bet you
dollars to donuts when you get men in the group, it will become much more 'Let's have a golf tournament, let's have a tennis
tournament, let's ....' You know ...." (corporate-government

relations official). It is not that the Tax Alliance women shy away from traditionally male sport activities at the retreat, but the competitive aspect is downplayed and even joked about. Some of the women I spoke with acknowledge the need to learn competitive sports in order to be able to "play with the boys," and are grateful that the retreat provides a "safe" place to learn: "I always find very fascinating the women who want to penetrate this dirty joke-fart-and-scratch male domain. And I think, deep down, it doesn't help you because they don't want you there and so it is kind of a 'Catch 22.' But if you want to learn how to play golf, thank God there is a Tax Alliance so you can go out and make a total fool of yourself. It helps you to play golf with some of the Members [of Congress], you know" (corporate-government relations official). It is evident from the language used to describe sport activities and "tournaments," and the nature of the awards presentations, that the Tax Alliance women work at downplaying the competitive aspect at the retreat.[5]

The Tax Alliance women clearly believe that the "special" quality of the organization and retreat enables them to develop close relationships. One Senate aide notes that, in part, this is because, for women, the "boundaries aren't quite so rigid" between family and work; they can "get in close" with other women right off the bat. "You know," she says, "we are a lot more likely to talk about kids or talk about the clothes you are wearing or whatever than with men you don't know very well. Once you get in closer, and it is someone that I do have a more friendly kind of a business relationship with, it seems to me that the boundaries aren't quite so rigid."

As stated by a corporate-government affairs official, the blurring of the family-work boundary "tends to soften relationships": "You have got enough social activities so that you can get to know somebody as a human being and enough substance to make it worthwhile and valuable to both people. And these things [retreats] are very family oriented. I think, you know, when you include family in these things, that tends to soften relationships compared with the sort of sports-oriented focus of the male-dominated retreats of the past."

Ironically, it is the "family oriented" nature of the Tax Alliance retreat that provides the seventeen male guests in attendance with access to government representatives they otherwise would not have. Many of the men who accompanied their wives or partners work as Washington corporate consultants and lawyers. Like the Tax Alliance women, these men attend formal sessions, banquets, dinners, and participate in sports activities.[6] But, for the Tax Alliance women, there is a distinct difference between the inclusion of men as "guests" and men as "members." As long as men are guests, the women are able to control with whom they interact; for example, through formal seating arrangements at dinner.[7] More importantly, according to the women, even though male partners are in attendance, the "special" character of the group is maintained.

The Tax Alliance women argue that they develop "deep" and "personal" friendships with business and government representatives that "you couldn't imagine happening" if men were members. According to one legislative aide, "There are a lot more opportunities to grow deeper friendships with the members of the Tax Alliance and also through non-work related social activities with each other. Sometimes I will see some of my Tax Alliance buddies there [at fundraisers] and that's just fun because they are friends as well as my colleagues but I will see people involved in the Tax Council who I just see as a face." Another staffer says: "While you can get the same kind of information perhaps from a mixed [gender] group, I am not sure the interaction would be the same. There are a number of both Hill people and off-the-Hill people that it has probably been easier to develop personal relationships with because of the fact that we are part of this group. It is already an interconnectedness, and so when we work issues together sometimes we are not quite as careful about communicating information back and forth." Further, they believe that men at the top levels of business and government could never develop the same kind of personal, long-lasting bonds that are developed between women in business and government at the Tax Alliance retreat:

> I could almost guarantee that the interaction is quite professional. It is not to say that they don't have personal friendships with these elected officials, but the men will have a much more sort of business-oriented focus, whereas the women who are interacting with staff are doing it not only for . . . . That they [men] are creating serious bonding friendships with these elected officials—they do happen but usually it is—I mean there is a limit there to what you are creating when you interact with elected officials because it is usually, "I know what we are here for. You are here to raise money or to advocate a position or an issue." I mean even at golf tournaments—those are neat situations and it is easy to get along with folks, but to say those men are creating long-lasting bonds and friendships is not [accurate]. (legislative aide, member of Congress)

According to the women interviewed, the Tax Alliance is the ideal networking organization because of its ability to combine deep, personal, serious friendships and business relationships—and men realize this fact and would love to be part of it: "I mean that's why they want in is because it is a good networking organization. They see that it is an opportunity to develop business and personal friendships, and that's why they want in. I think to the extent that they were participating, you know, they would be hoping to get the same kinds of things out of it—well, they would be hoping to get personal relationships that would then ultimately end up making it easier for them to get their business relationships done" (legislative aide, Senator).

Men are aware of the substantial benefits provided by the Tax Alliance women's "special" relationships. According to another legislative aide, "Men are jealous of our networking capability almost to the point that they tease us about it. I don't know if anybody told you some of the names."[8] A corporate government relations official says, similarly: "The Tax Alliance has actually created an interesting dynamic with its members. You feel like you are part of a club, and the men tax allies are resenting it now. They used to have their own, men-only groups, and they don't now. But this organization [Tax Alliance] has created a lot of interesting feelings among men tax professionals in the public sector and I think in the private sector too because the private sector tax lobbyists would love to have the relationships and access to these public sector tax professionals that we do." But because the Tax Alliance women use gender, and specifically femininity, in constructing their relationships, men could never form the same kinds of relationships. Moreover, were men to become members, the Tax Alliance would never be the same. The dominant sentiment is that the organization and retreat are "different" and "special," and the women would rather things remain just the way they are. And so they will—at least for the time being.

The ways in which gender is created and used by the women of the Tax Alliance, reproducing femininity through their relationships and activities while working hard to counter the characterization, seems to have two important outcomes. First, it helps the women in overcoming the second-class citizenship that led them to form the organization in the first place. It gives them credibility and leverage in relation to any men who might tend to exclude them. Second, it is ideal for strengthening business-government relations. The Tax Alliance women go out of their way to present themselves as serious, strong, and substantive—characteristics associated with men and masculinity. But it is not just a matter of appearance. They hold formal work sessions and luncheons, gathering and exchanging information and making their voices heard. They work extra hard at becoming technically expert and highly educated and informed. At the same time, the Tax Alliance women speak fondly of intimate, deep, personal relationships and the non-threatening, non-competitive, and safe environment that they have created. In terms of organizational and intra-organizational consequences, what could be a more ideal setting for solidifying business-government relations and securing business power in the political realm?

DOING GENDER AND DOING
CORPORATE POWER AT THE RETREAT

My participant observation research revealed that the Tax Alliance, a business-government policy discussion group that meets at off-the-record hotels and spas is, in many ways, a lot like male-dominated retreats and business policy groups. Much like Domhoff's description of the Bohemian Grove, the business-government partnership is reinforced and policy shaped through interactions, activities, ceremonies, and rituals that take place in the secluded setting of the Tax Alliance retreat. Events such as the Sequins Only Banquet and Awards ceremony contribute, ideologically, to the general sense of business-government cohesion. The business-government partnership is also strengthened through participants' overlapping career paths. The public sector women at the Tax Alliance retreat work hard to establish close relationships with, and earn the favor of, corporate women for the purpose of career advancement.

The activities, rituals, ceremonies, and interactions that take place at these policy group retreats contribute significantly to a general shift in which women have become an increasingly important part of the policy-planning process in the United States. Through the close bonds that are formed, and the formal sessions held each day, business and government participants share important information concerning policy issues. At the retreat, business is provided with a heads up on what government is doing, or thinking about, before policy is made. More importantly, because of their "special" partnership, business has privileged access to the government representatives and the legislative process.

The ways in which the Tax Alliance women do and use gender produces an ideal environment for solidifying the business-government partnership and business power. Gender, and specifically femininity, is highly salient at the retreat largely because the Tax Alliance was founded, and still operates, on the premise that women (in response to their exclusion from men's networks) could and would help one another access and share information, provide career advice and support, and provide a non-threatening "safe" haven for their voices to be heard. Women do femininity in the organization and at the retreat as part of a gender hegemony, whereby the gendered characteristics and relations they describe are consistent with current hegemonic femininity (Connell 1995, 472). They teach, help, nurture, and comfort each other. But women not only "do" femininity at the Tax Alliance retreat; they "call it up as a driving force" (Scott 1999, 73). They emphasize the caring, trusting, relationships and non-threatening, non-competitive activities and environment that are created at the retreat and are what makes the event so beneficial and special to them. They "mobilize" femininity much as men construct and use masculinity— to resist and bond. As part of their attempt to contest masculinity and resist and combat perceived oppression, they affirm the "different" (feminine) character of their relations and retreat, describing their relationships as far more "intimate, deep, and personal" than men's (Martin 2001). They construct and use femininity in their relationships and activities to provide comfort, cohesion, and strength. It could be argued that the retreat provides an ideal setting for calling up femininity because it takes place in a leisure setting, far from male-dominated work organizations where the use of femininity to solidify relationships is likely to be devalued.

Whether the women of the Tax Alliance in fact form deeper, more intimate and personal kinds of relations and create a less threatening and competitive environment than do men and male policy groups is an empirical question that this research cannot answer. What is important is that the Tax Alliance women believe this to be the case. That they welcomed me as a full participant at their retreat, and later in Washington greeted me with hugs and took me to lunch, could be seen as indications of the trust, safety, and mutual understanding that they perceive exists between women.

The Tax Alliance women reconstruct and use femininity through their interactions and activities at the retreat, but at the same time avoid any association with women's groups or women's issues and the perception that they are "just a bunch of women" getting together to socialize. It is very important to the Tax Alliance women that they be seen by others not as expressive but as rational, technical, and instrumental, terms used to characterize the work men do in a capitalist bureaucracy. They take great pride in the fact that they are an organization of women who specialize in the "important," traditionally male policy areas of tax and social security. They are all highly credentialed, with advanced law and business degrees from Georgetown and Harvard. Most of the Tax Alliance women have acquired a wealth of technical expertise and information in the areas of taxes, social security, and health care and are confident and highly adept public speakers. They hold formal sessions and produce volumes of paperwork for distribution at the retreat, in large part to "prove" to male colleagues and bosses that they are doing "serious" and "substantive" work. In their effort to publicly downplay the feminine character of their retreat, they call up masculinity.

Smith (1984, 398) argues that gender is a part of class op-pression; the ideal construct of males as rational, impersonal, ob-jective, and unemotional is tied to structures of power. Where power and rationality are connected with capitalism and bu-reaucracy, rationality emerges as a specialized and discrete arena of exercising power. Women work hard at becoming highly cre-dentialed and technically expert in order to gain competency and credibility in the rational sphere. At the same time, through their interactions and activities, they pride themselves in hav-ing special ability and strength in the "expressive" or "personal" sphere. As these women reproduce the rational-expressive di-chotomy, they reproduce gender difference, which justifies keep-ing men in positions of power and paying women less.

As the Tax Alliance women do and use gender, they pro-duce what is possibly the most highly competent, effective busi-ness-government networking group in Washington. Moreover, because the Tax Alliance is viewed as "credible" among those at all levels of business and government, the women are "highly networked" with women and men on key committees and in key administrative departments in government. And because many view the organization and its activities as a "kind of affir-mative action," it is "impervious to attack." Thus business-gov-ernment relations are likely to benefit from the Tax Alliance and its retreat for a long time to come.

CHAPTER 5

The Costs and Benefits
of Family Ties

ALTHOUGH RESEARCHERS HAVE examined the relationship between gender and work networks (Aldrich and Reese 1994; Brass 1985, 1992), few have included the effects of family relations on work networks in their analyses. The social science literature that does exist in this area largely suggests that family ties limit women's opportunities to form work networks. For example, researchers have argued that professional women who are wives and mothers may "pay the price of being defined as uncommitted" to their careers (Saltzman Chafetz 1997; see also Lorber 1989). With regard to ties with those in higher-level positions, Moore (1987) finds that married men with children name more advisors as "close ties" than women in the same situation.

As more women become involved in corporate lobbying, and because work networks are crucial in establishing strong business-government ties, it is important to ask whether and how family ties affect work experiences and interactions. This chapter examines gender differences in family relations and responsibilities among corporate lobbyists and explores the effects of these differences on work networks. To what extent do marriage and family create obstacles to interacting with key people in government and business? Are married women, or women with children, limited in the particular kinds of networking in which they engage? For example, are they less likely to attend social events as compared with talk on the phone with key people in business and government? More generally, for both corporate lobbyists and legislative staff, how does the character of women's family connections limit or enhance their chances to establish workplace interactions?

FAMILY TIES: EXPRESSIVE OR INSTRUMENTAL?

Much of the work and family literature argues that women are limited in the workplace as a result of an unequal division of domestic labor. Researchers generally agree that women shoulder the brunt of a variety of domestic work, ranging from direct forms of housework and childcare (Coverman 1989; Ferree 1991; Manke et al. 1994; Pleck 1985; Saltzman Chafetz 1997; Shelton and John 1993; Vanek 1983; Wharton 1994), kinkeeping (DiLeonardo 1987; Gerstel and Gallagher 1990), and the emotion work involved in all these activities (Hochschild 1983). Even when employed, women's share of family work far exceeds men's (Coverman 1989; Pleck 1985; Reskin and Padavic 2002; South and Spitze 1994).

It has been argued further that dual-career couples negotiate a relatively egalitarian division of labor in the home (Hertz 1986). Moreover, Gerstel and Gross suggest that some married women professionals might be more productive in their professions than their single counterparts. But these researchers also argue that "typically these women feel desperately pressed for time, giving up their own leisure and sleep to meet demands of both employment and family. Unlike men, these women discover that their job and family constantly intrude on each other" (Gerstel and Gross 1989, 107, 108). Others suggests that, even though professional women may have relatively egalitarian ideologies, "surface ideology," actual feelings, and, ultimately, practice may collide (Hochschild 1983; see also Yogev 1984).

Not only is family work typically viewed by social scientists as limiting women's success in the workplace, but relations in the home tend not to be characterized as useful in general. This is the case regardless of women's social class. Although only certain kinds of relations in the workplace are likely to be labeled "expressive" ("friendships" with other women, for example), most relations outside the workplace, and particularly those in the home, are characterized this way (Scott 1996). The classic argument is that the spheres women and men occupy are accompanied by distinct and different roles; specifically women's expressive specialization in the home and men's instrumental specialization in the marketplace (Parsons and Bales 1955).

An exception to this "family-as-constraint" perspective is provided by social capital theorists, who argue that family ties are potentially instrumental. Marceau (1989, 141), who studied elite families, notes that ties to well-connected relatives are important for providing useful information and resources. "Not only are the actual contacts important," she says, but "the claims and obligations of kinship work to multiply the economic resources to which couples in this milieu have access and on which they can call." The volume of social capital possessed by any particular group member thus depends on the breadth of the network of links that he or she can effectively mobilize and on the volume of capital (economic, cultural, and symbolic) possessed by each individual in the group to whom he or she is linked (Bourdieu 1980, 3 in Marceau 1989, 141).

The "family-as-social-capital" argument has been quite successfully applied to the study of class issues, but has rarely been used to understand the connection between family and workplace structures and relations for women specifically. It is plausible that the family ties of women corporate lobbyists provide social capital; they may establish instrumental relations through well-connected family. The social capital provided by family ties may be particularly important in government affairs

work given the significance of networking with those in business and government.

Drawing from interviews, participant-observation, and survey
data, this chapter examines the family ties of women lobbyists and
other corporate-government relations officials. As more women
enter the area of corporate-government affairs, which requires a
substantial amount of "interaction work" and also demands substantial time and flexibility on the part of the worker, it becomes
important to ask about the effects of family relations. How do
family relations differ for women and men government affairs
managers? Are married women and women with children disproportionately burdened in the home, compared with their male
counterparts and with other women who are free of family ties.
Second, how does women's family status influence their interactions with key people in business and government? Finally, how
do women's and men's family ties provide the social and political
capital that affect their experiences and opportunities at work?

Marriage, Children, and Family Work

Survey data reveals that, although most government relations officials who represent corporations are married and have
children, women are significantly more likely to be single and
childless than their male counterparts. Among those with children, women are significantly more likely to have only one child
and to have younger children (under age six) living at home.
Particularly among older respondents—those who are forty-six
or older—women are significantly more likely than men to have
younger children. Over half these women have children who are
twelve or under, compared with only 17 percent of men. A third
of women in this age bracket, compared with none of the men,
report having children under six years of age at home.

This profile of government relations managers is compatible
with trends reported elsewhere. Women in high-level professional
positions are more likely than their male counterparts to be single

and childless. This is especially the case among women who are older and more likely to be entrenched in their careers. It is not necessarily that these professional women never marry—they may be less likely than their male counterparts to remarry. Why is this the case? Partly it is because, for women, being married and having children mean a substantial time and energy commitment, one that some professional women are hesitant to take on. Research finds that, although less work is done in the home as more women enter the workforce, gender inequality in the division of labor remains. Women continue to spend at least three times as many hours in domestic work as men, even when employed in high-level, demanding careers (Bianchi, et al. 2000; Coverman 1989; Hochschild 1989; Vanek 1983).

Married women government relations officials spend far more time on family work than their colleagues. Married women spend forty-four hours per week on housework and childcare; single women are next with eighteen hours per week, then married men with seventeen hours, and lastly single men with sixteen hours. Although marriage, in itself, does not seem to disproportionately burden women in terms of the amount of time spent specifically on housework, the onset of children makes a profound difference in the amount of time married women spend on family work. Married women with children spend, on average, three times as much time doing childcare as men in government affairs; thirty-six hours per week for women, compared with eleven hours for married men. Moreover, the gap between women and men remains regardless of whether there are one, two, or three or more children in the household. But it is not just the amount of time spent doing housework and childcare that separates women and men government relations managers. For women government relations officials in business and government, family work and government relations work overlaps to a greater extent in time and space; for men, the boundaries are much clearer.

NOT-SO-SEPARATE SPHERES:
TIME, SPACE, AND THE WEEKEND SHIFT

Interviews with women and men in Washington, D.C., and participant observation data at the Tax Alliance retreat reveal that, while women government relations officials do a "second shift" day in and day out, men do a "weekend shift" (Hochschild 1989; Manke et al. 1994).[1] The men interviewed report that they do not generally see family work as their responsibility during the week, but increase their workload on the weekends. Several men mentioned the work they do on the weekend as the most significant part of their household participation. One corporate government relations vice president reported that "on weekends—I have a six-year-old and a four-year-old—so the weekends are usually my days for the boys and Mommy gets a break. Household chores? I do the dishes; I cook—On the weekend I do the cooking, so that would be all the time on the weekend. During the week my wife cooks, I do the dishes. If I cook, she does the dishes. I guess I don't do any other housework." This weekend work does not typically include a great deal of "down-and-dirty" housekeeping, but consists mostly of spending time with the children (for example, doing recreational activities— one man spoke of attending basketball games with his sons) and perhaps doing some or all of the cooking.

Even when it comes to the work of birthing, men are reluctant to take time from paid work, unless the birth of a child falls on or around the weekend. One government relations manager notes that, luckily, one of his children was born on a Saturday— he "had the day off already." Another recollects the following: "I stayed home with my wife. Let me put it this way: when the first one was born, my wife was in labor for thirty hours. He was born on a Thursday so I didn't go back to work till the following Monday. The second was born on Friday night and I think I may have taken Monday or Tuesday off."

Men separate paid work and family work by time (weekends versus the "workweek") and also space:

> My husband is into hockey himself and so he spends sizeable chunks of time with the boys, but once hockey is done, he goes out to his living room and he reads his books or, you know, turns on the TV and watches his sports or does whatever he needs to do and he pretty much is done, you know. I can't read a book, I can't—I can read the paper maybe, but I am usually interacting with the kids or doing some kind of homework or whatever, or interacting with them somehow—and Matt will come home and he will grab his dinner. He will go upstairs to his little hideaway room, and he will watch TV and eat and maybe we will see him during the course of the evening. (legislative aide, member of Congress)

Not only does Matt separate himself physically from the routine work of housekeeping and childcare, but has also been given ownership of the space and all objects in it, which implies entitlement and earned privacy.

In contrast, women's family and paid government relations work overlap to the extent that "doing labor" takes on a whole new meaning. One legislative aide interviewed told me the story of a female congressional staffer who "was in labor, and her boss called her wanting to know about an appropriations bill. You know, in labor at the hospital, and her boss just decides to call her up. She is sitting here doing an amendment as she is in labor." Another woman who is a top aide to a Senator describes family-work overlap this way: "There was one time when I had a sick kid and a husband out of town, and we were getting ready for a mark-up. I brought him in with a little bucket, and he was puking in the corner, and we got through the mark-up. I mean you do what you need to do, but he (Senator X) was willing to take a chance on me in doing that, and there are a lot of Members who are not." In these cases, birthing and nursing (primarily women's work) are not seen as "real" work, and thus these staffers are viewed as "free" to work on writing legislation—real work.

These data, taken together, suggest that women, especially married women with children, are substantially burdened compared with other government affairs managers—they are the people who do most in the home, particularly during the work-week when most dinners and fundraisers (for congressional and senatorial candidates) take place. And in both time and space, women indicate that they do more "interaction" work at home, and there is more work-family overlap for women than their male counterparts. All of this suggests that women with families have less "free" time to form work ties. How then do women compete with men in forming and maintaining the relationships with key people in business and government that are so necessary to maintain strong business-government bonds?

FAMILY TIES AND WORK NETWORKS

Women on the Hill who work as legislative aides are more likely than corporate women to be single and childless. They also tend to be at earlier stages in their career and younger. The single women I interviewed, most of whom are legislative aides, see themselves as having more "freedom" to network than those who are "attached." This is the potential scenario described by one single woman:"[If] I have a family, I have to go home, so you are stuck with doing the Saturday evening or the early morning event. You know I can't go because I have to drop off the kids. I can't do this because I have to pick them up at the playgroup. So it is definitely ... especially here (in her office) where the work day is not 9 to 5. You know sometimes it is 7:30 to 9:00 at night, and you are expected to do things after 5:00 that are definitely part of the job. In this office most of us are young and single and unattached with no children" (legislative aide, member of Congress). Another single women says:

If I was married there would probably be a problem a lot of times when you have to work late, when you have to hang around the Hill, and you always have to be in really early. I get up between 7:00 and 7:30, and I get home between 6:30 and 7:00 at night, 11 or sometimes after. You go to dinners sometimes. It doesn't affect me at all. Probably I would have a hard time if I had someone who was depending on me at home.

Q: But it's not an issue for you?

A: No. That's what keeps me from getting married . . .

For married women and mothers, who do a second shift and for whom the work-family overlap is significant, "freedom" to do any kind of concentrated networking is significantly limited in several ways. For most of the government relations officials in this study, it means scheduling meetings in and around the space of the nine-to-five work day.

A New Culture: The Breakfast Club

According to interviewees, coinciding with the increased pace of women's entry into corporate lobbying in the last couple of decades has been a gradual but nevertheless dramatic change in the culture and character of networking in Washington, D.C. For instance, although it is still important to show up at large fundraisers (with contribution check in hand), corporate and legislative officials are finding small, intimate breakfasts and luncheons a better use of their precious time. As a legislative aide notes, "Fund-raisers are changing. There are a lot more breakfast and luncheon fund-raisers. I think it reflects a little bit more of everyone trying to be conscious [of family responsibilities] but I don't know." Whether the change from the big evening fundraiser (or "cattle calls") to the more intimate breakfast or luncheon gatherings is directly related to the entry of women into staff and corporate positions and gender-based inequality in family work is a question this research cannot definitively answer. However, interview comments and survey data suggest a relationship between the two. In the context of talking about family responsibilities and networking, one legislative aide said, "I try to avoid after-work events like the plague. I mean I'll occasionally do a dinner if I absolutely feel like it is essential, but I don't do the round of, you know, receptions and networking kinds of things and stuff like that. If I can't do it for lunch or breakfast, I try not to schedule it."

Survey data show that married women who work as corporate-government relations manages are as likely as men to network with those at all levels of business and government. They are as likely as others to talk with staff members and other government relations managers, and top corporate executives. They are also as likely as others to share meals with those at all levels from among their colleagues as well as those at the top in business and government—corporate heads, legislators, other legislative staff, and government relations managers. But there is a gender difference in the timing and context of their interaction.

Married women and women with children are less likely to network in non-work settings (attending a concert, theater, or sporting event) with legislators and staff members. Except for work history (worked for a legislator), being a married women is the only factor that affects this kind of non-work interaction with those in government, controlling for the effects of other variables. Married women government affairs managers are, however, as likely as anyone else to go to breakfast, lunch, or dinner with legislators, staff members, and other government relations officials.

Although socializing in informal settings—playing golf, going to the theater or concerts—is important in establishing relationships and a common culture, socializing at these kinds of events is not the only, nor necessarily the most important, setting where business is done and connections are established.

Government relations officials note that sharing a small, intimate breakfast or lunch provides an ideal way to "get the ear" of a legislator or staff member.

This does not mean that luncheons, breakfasts, or dinners are necessarily arranged for the purpose of accomplishing business, or even that the focus of the meeting is a particular issue. In fact, little time may be spent specifically talking about business, as one woman government relations manager notes: "I can go to lunch with people and take two minutes of their time talking about my issue, spend the rest of my time catching up with what's new. Some of those people are my best friends on the Hill. I see them personally, socially, and they're very good to me. They are always there to help me with my issues. But I don't think you have to spend two hours of somebody's time groaning and beating an issue into their heads."

Although it is likely that this cultural change in networking on the Hill has been in part driven by the structural limitations imposed mostly on women by the work-family nexus, interviewees note that men also enjoy the benefits. As one legislative aide notes, "I can't imagine it as anything other than women in the vanguard, but men are agreeing. It is not like they are resisting this. We are hearing guys who are the heads of Washington offices say, 'Hey, I got baseball, I got soccer, I got to be home'— so they work it out with their offices." Even those at the top do not seem to be resisting; as one legislative aide notes, "The dinners are, you know, we promise to get you out of there by . . . If it starts at six, we promise to get you out at eight, and generally the Members appreciate that. They don't want to hang around any longer than moms and dads with kids at home, so it is not— I don't think it is really a disadvantage." To the contrary, this new "culture" of networking works to the advantage of everyone. It provides an ideal context for business-government relations to flourish, and additional time at home for men and women who represent these institutions.

BUYING TIME AND WORKING HARD

Even with this cultural shift in the timing and context of networking in Washington, establishing and maintaining bonds requires a substantial amount of time and effort. Most of the women interviewed said that women have to do more, work harder, "just to be judged as equal." As one corporate lobbyist says, "For a woman in any role in the corporation, you have to prove yourself just to be in, and then you have to work twice as hard to show that you can do the job. You are not given that. You have to prove you can do the job. And then you've got to be better." The quantitative data show that, in fact, women in government affairs put in more hours than their male colleagues at home *and* in the workplace. Women in government affairs put in a "second shift" at home, working, on average, twenty-three more hours than their male counterparts each week. At the same time, they report working just as many hours as men in their government relations jobs (fifty-one hours per week for both women and men, on average).[2]

It is doubtful women would be able to maintain their professional relations, much less get ahead, without some sort of paid help in the home. Women in government relations not only earn substantial salaries, but tend to be married to those with high incomes as well. The average family income of women government affairs managers is $125,000–$149,000 (over $175,000 for the top twenty-fifth percentile). Unlike those in some other occupations, these women can afford quality care for their children and at least some assistance with household responsibilities.

Hired workers in turn help enable these women maintain the networks necessary to nurture their high-paying careers. When asked how family responsibilities affect her ability to form relations with key people in government and business, one woman government relations manager reports that "it's real tough. I have two kids, a one-year-old and a four-year-old. I have a very understanding husband; he's an attorney and he's got a very demanding job. I have a very good housekeeper, who I pay a pretty penny to. That takes a big chunk of your salary when you're doling out $25,000 a year on childcare."

Although the majority of government relations officials have some sort of paid help, a significantly higher proportion of women than men report having hired help. Approximately three-quarters of married women, with and without children, have paid help, compared with about half of the married men. Questionnaire data show that women government affairs managers are more apt than their male counterparts to be married to people with high-level, demanding, jobs, particularly in business. Paid help becomes the only alternative if they are to have the "free" time required for developing and maintaining the network that are so essential for strong business-government relations. As one woman government relations official said, " I know one woman [who is] on the PAC Committee who has three children, and another one who is pregnant with a second, both with full careers at good levels—up there within the management scale. You have to look at those kinds of people and say, it can be done. But their personal lives are hairy. One woman has a full-time housekeeper. You'd have to do things like that if you wanted to carry on."

FAMILY TIES AS SOCIAL CAPITAL

Although women put in a substantial amount of time doing and managing family work, the effects of women's family ties can be seen as paradoxical. They are burdensome and at the same time provide social capital, linking women to a broad network of key people who could provide useful information, as well as practical, career-related resources and assistance. Smith-Lovin and McPherson (1993, 235) point to research that shows that "women are much more likely to know people through their husbands' coworker networks than men are to know their wives' work friends," implying that "women benefit more from their spouses' network positions than do men; women use their husbands' work contacts to extend their own ties." Other evidence, however, suggests that the "contacts women make through their husbands may be less useful to women in work-related spheres, and supportive only of their roles as wives." Although it may be true that for some women the networks they develop through their spouses support their roles as wives, in the case of high-level professional women they may also provide useful work-related links.

Forty-two percent of the women surveyed report that their husbands are top corporate executives, lawyers, or consultants. In contrast, only three percent of the men report that their wives occupy such positions. Thirty-eight percent of the men, compared with two percent of the women, report their spouses' occupations as either "housewife" (their term; no women reported being married to "househusbands") or "no occupation." Another eighteen percent of the men are married to women with flexible jobs, or jobs that require less than full-time schedules, such as teacher, interior decorator, or realtor.

On one hand, women who are married to men with jobs that are relatively inflexible may by limited in terms of their own flexibility and the amount of time they can devote to developing work networks. Research shows that the time women spend on family work is significantly related to the character of husbands' jobs. In her study of women in real estate, Carol Wharton (1994, 197) interviewed women who note that in order to successfully combine their careers and family responsibilities, it is "essential for husbands to do an equal share of domestic labor." Wharton (1994, 198) argues that a factor contributing to husbands' sharing more of the household labor is their occupation or work schedule. Husbands with flexible occupations or work schedules are likely to participate more; looked at the other way around, husbands' inflexible occupations offer one explanation for their lack of involvement.

An analysis of average hours spent doing childcare indeed shows that spouses' occupation is a significant factor when controlling for other variables; the more inflexible the spouses' occupation, the more hours per week respondents spend on childcare. The only other significant factor is the presence of young children (under thirteen years old) in the household. Further analysis suggests that the effects of spouses' occupations are different for women and men. Occupation of spouse is found to be significant for women but not for men, controlling for other factors. For men, the occupations of their wives would probably not significantly reduce the number of hours spent on childcare—men's level of participation is relatively low whether their wives have flexible occupations or not. But for women, who bear the brunt of work in the home, the flexibility of their husbands' occupations matters.

Although these ties may impose limitations for women in government affairs in that their husbands are potentially less likely to contribute in the home, they present an interesting paradox. Family ties, particularly with those in key positions in business and government, provide several important kinds of resources. First, they extend the networks of women in government affairs. Women in government affairs, through their husbands or other family members, meet and establish social bonds with people whom they might not otherwise establish relationships—bonds that can be very helpful in future business dealings and in establishing credibility. According to one congressional aide:

> I work for a Republican and [my husband] works for a Democrat, so it really makes it interesting, you know, the people that we will meet and that kind of thing. I think it certainly helped because I have met a lot of other people that I probably otherwise wouldn't have met that have then come back on a business level and they already know me,

and I think it helps give me a little bit of credibility in some of those areas because you know his friend that I have met at other—that have come over to the house for whatever—and then they are also lobbyists and need to call me about something, and they already know who I am, and that sort of thing. Or we will be at home and will be talking about an issue, and he will say, "You can call so and so; they talked to me about that last week."

Another well-known and highly respected legislative aide says, "I have a brother who is involved with government affairs work. I mean the two of us use each other constantly, you know, as far as information we are trying to get and stuff like that. I think family is good." This woman's brother and one of her sisters are government relations managers at top corporations in Washington. These familial connections are important in broadening her network and gaining information: "My sister works for [XX] Corporation and her CEO came in to visit, and I said 'Oh, you know Mary is my sister and my brother also used to work for [XX],' and he was like, 'Oh well, I know them and I know your dad,' and so immediately we had . . . I mean this is a Top 10 company, and he immediately has a better relationship with me because of the small network that we have. So I think it has helped me" (legislative aide, member of Congress).

There are many similar examples from the interviews of how women's family ties are used as social and political capital. Another woman who represents a major corporation in Washington describes how her husband's "political contacts" have provided her with an extended social network of ties with key people in the political realm:

My husband does that same thing that I do, although he does it in a law firm. He runs the law firm, a Philadelphia-based firm. He runs the Washington office and he does

lobby. He used to be a real lawyer but now he is very politically active, and he has been in the lobbying end of the
practice of law for over twelve years.

Q: Do you think that your husband has provided you with resources in terms of networking?

A: Yes, but mostly because of his political ties. His political life
is very active and so instead of the sort of corporate kind
of thing, it is mostly political contacts—political contacts
and friendships that he has made over the years and because he was a political party leader. The social contacts
that we have made through that aspect of our lives, the
political end of our lives, which is very active in party
politics. You get to know on a different, from a different
angle than a professional relationship where you are talking issues all the time.

Another significant way women broaden their network ties is
through their husbands' social club memberships. Although there
is some evidence that women are being sponsored for membership in social clubs (for example, one woman said she is being
sponsored for membership in the Congressional Country Club
by another woman), women are often excluded from this realm
of networking. However, several women interviewed noted that
they became involved in social clubs through their husband:

Now my husband—we belong and participate; so maybe I
should qualify that.

Q: In terms of sponsorship, then . . . through your husband?

A: Club members work in the same field that he does and they
had to sponsor us.

Q: Was your sponsor work-related?

A: Yes. A lot of times there's great crossover in this town (D. C.)
. . . I find little separation; your life is mixed with the same
people you're working with.

Q: Was this a manager or legislator?

A: One guy [who sponsored us] had a top spot in his trade association, and the other guy had a top spot in his [trade] group.

Through their husbands' social club memberships, women interact with top-level people who potentially provide them with
information or career-related opportunities or both.

Children may also provide opportunities to develop work
networks in various ways. One woman government relations
manager notes: "There are summer conferences that bring together state legislative officials, so at those conferences, you get
to meet the state senator as well as his wife and his three kids.
That has been very helpful in terms of a network at the state
level, where you can't get to all these state capitals, and not being able to go as often as I used to. At least I get to see people
once a year, and they know my husband. I don't have children—I bring one of my nieces. So there's a social element to
it, very family oriented. It's nice." That this woman substitutes
her niece for her own children is an indication of the significance of family status, particularly parenthood, for establishing
work connections.

It is not just women who benefit from family ties; husbands
also benefit. As discussed in the previous chapter, husbands ac-
company their wives to exclusive retreats where key people in
business and government are present. Is it because they will be
lonely at home while their wives are soaking in the spa? Perhaps. But it is more likely because of the important information
and opportunity to form bonds with key people in business and
government that are available to them simply by virtue of their
familial ties. The women interviewed in Washington also spoke
of the benefits their husbands reap from their network ties.

According to one interviewee, a corporate woman, it is most
beneficial, both to the family economy and to effective network
building, for the wife to "stay on the Hill," and the husband to
"go downtown," particularly if they work in the same issue area

(e.g., taxes, health care, education). She noted two reasons for this: "One, if they are in the same issue area, it helps the man downtown. Two, it is harder for a woman to get a top-paying job in a firm downtown relative to her husband, and so to maximize that sort of economic strength of that familial unit, it is better for women to stay on the Hill and her husband go downtown. And then you have the federal government . . . with the passage of time women are moving up to having very senior positions in federal agencies . . ." (corporate-government relations manager). This arrangement ensures that men move up within corporations or lobbing firms ("hired guns" as some call them), owing their advancement at least partly to the information and influence gleaned from their wives' connections in government: "I just think of Herman. He has been the managing partner of a law firm downtown. It makes more sense you know—he could get that big job and, you know, Barbara (his wife, a top legislative aide) . . . One looks, and it makes a lot of sense for that family unit to be divided the way it is. It benefits him immensely because of her relationships, you know, and his opportunities to network see" (legislative aide, member of Congress). Given persistent ideologies that portray women as primary homemaker and childcare provider, and given the significant inequality in the amount of time and energy women and men actually spend on family work, it is not particularly surprising that, even among these high-paid women, men are still seen as the person whose job is to make it to the top at all costs:

> There is a bunch of women, we go one on one with the hired guns, and those are mostly male. If you are a hired gun in this town, you are out every night. That's the very nature of it, so . . . at what level do you want to play the game? I think there's a group of women and men who have realized the tradeoff and have said, "I don't want to pay the price." I think it is harder in some ways for women because,

you know, we are in many ways sort of the vanguard, and so we have had to push harder to gain that credibility to be recognized in the job market. At some point you got to pay the price. You know, you are going against men who are paying that price, you know being out there and building those relationships, because so much of politics is personal that you just got to do it . . . (corporate-government relations official)

Family ties need not be so directly related to work ties in order to serve as a resource. In general, those who work in government affairs, whether in the corporate or government realms, share a social world. Particularly in Washington, they "go through weddings, births, deaths, the human cycle, and the people you draw on for surviving this are the people in the same community." Government relations officials meet their future spouses through their work networks. They see each other at the same restaurants, stores, health clubs, and hair salons. Their children attend the same schools and daycare centers. It is not surprising, then, that women and men who work in business and government in Washington derive social and political capital through their family ties.

Social scientists have mostly focused on the benefits professional men receive through family ties, specifically from relations with their wives. The literature has accurately identified the work done by women in the home as essential in the maintenance of men's careers. The data collected for this research supports the argument that men reap considerable benefits from women's work in the home. Additionally, wives and sisters who work for members of Congress, Senators, and government agencies provide critical information and connections that benefit men enormously in the business realm. At the same time, there are significant costs involved in women's family ties. The women interviewed for this study say that they work harder than men, sometimes taking extraordinary measures, to be seen as "credible" in their jobs, while at the same time acting as responsible parents and wives. On top of this, they do considerable emotion work in their effort to "do it all," and do it well. One legislative aide spoke of the tremendous "guilt" carried by her women friends who feel they to blame for their children's difficulties or deficiencies. Understood from a gender perspective, the cleanliness of the home and the health, welfare, and appearance of children are generally viewed as a "reflection on women's competence as a 'wife and mother'—but not men's competence as a 'husband and father'" (Bianchi, et al. 2000, 176).

It is the case that there are significant costs to establishing work networks that are embedded in women's family ties, but in focusing on the limitations, we fail to recognize the potential advantages women gain through their family ties. Like men, women in corporate-government affairs derive significant social capital from their family ties. Women are potentially even more advantaged than their male counterparts in this regard, since their husbands (and brothers, fathers) are far more likely to occupy positions in business and government than are the wives of male government relations officials. Through their husbands, brothers, and fathers, women's work networks are broadened, and, as such, they are exposed to information and influence they might otherwise not have.

In addition, there is some evidence from this study that women's family ties are perhaps driving a change in the Washington networking culture. As argued in the last chapter, women's networking is important for maintaining strong business-government relations, and the heads of business and government (typically men) know it. Intimate breakfasts and luncheons not only accommodate women's family responsibilities, but they also provide an ideal place to build strong business-government ties.

On one hand, the data suggest that it is more difficult for women in corporate-government affairs than their male counterparts to combine family responsibilities and work relations. Women government affairs managers are significantly less likely than men to be married and have children. When they do have children, women are significantly more likely to have fewer than men. Moreover, the data suggest that women are less likely than men to remarry. One implication of these findings is that, in order to succeed in their jobs, women must be relatively free of family ties, whereas men are able to be married, have children, and still do their jobs. An examination of family work provides further support for the claim that family ties present a greater obstacle for women than men in government affairs. The data show that, even when outside help is employed, family work is essentially in the hands of women. Corresponding with the research of others, survey results indicate that married women spend considerably more time on this work than others; at least three times as many hours as anyone else. Moreover, a significant proportion of women in government affairs are married to men with inflexible, high-level jobs, which significantly affects the amount of time they spend on family work. We would expect that because women corporate-government affairs managers, particularly those with children, do far more in the home than their male counterparts and other women, and are married to men with jobs that prevent them assuming this responsibility, they would be substantially limited in terms of opportunities and rewards, and the social relations that structure them.

There are some significant costs embedded in these results. For women who combine raising families with being a full-time government affairs official, there are limitations in the character and context of their work ties. Married women are less apt to talk with legislators, and less apt to network in informal, social contexts (attending a sports event, concert, the theater) with those in business and government, thereby limiting their opportunities and resources.

But in other ways the data show that family ties are not as limiting as might be expected. Although women are less likely than men to be married and have children, the majority of women in government affairs are married and have children, suggesting that women are far from abandoning the ideal of successfully combining work and family. Furthermore, survey results indicate that neither marriage nor motherhood limits the most kinds of networking. Married women are as likely as others to talk and share meals with those in business and government, and to attend social events with their colleagues in government relations management. Married women and women with children are less likely to attend social events with those at the top, but, given the shift in the culture of networking, at least in Washington, this type of networking is perhaps taking on less importance as a routine way for business and government to exchange ideas and information.

There is also some evidence that women in government affairs, in both the business and government realms, may even benefit from their family ties by gaining social capital. Husbands, brothers, fathers, and other family members connect them to key people in business and government. Their social networks are therefore broadened through these family ties. These networks potentially provide important information about what is happening in the business and legislative realms, information that can be critical if one is to be a successful government affairs official. Additionally, family ties also provide women with information and access to jobs in business and government.

There is no doubt that women's family ties not only impose limitations in terms of the types of activities women engage in and networks they form outside the home, because of time or normative constraints, but also affect the treatment of women in the workplace by virtue of their ideological status as "wives" and "mothers." But family ties might not be as costly as the literature would lead us to believe. Women work very hard to keep up work networks and at the same time maintain family ties. They use their family ties as a resource to extend their work networks, schedule breakfast and luncheon meetings, and find occasional "safe havens" like the Tax Alliance Retreat as places where they can "get away from it all," relax, and informally network with their friends in business and government. As Smith-Lovin and McPherson (1993, 245) noted almost a decade ago, " . . . women may not end up in a different world, just a more crowded one," which, in the end, may help business-government relations more than anything.

CHAPTER 6

Women, Corporate Lobbying, and Power

WOMEN'S PRESENCE ON the lobbying scene in Washington and elsewhere in the country is undeniable. The "bastions of cigar-smoking dinosaurs," as one corporate lobbyist put it, are nearly extinct. It is no longer unusual to see women lobbyists networking with legislators and staffers and arguing their cases in the halls of Congress, at restaurants, and on the golf course. Women have fast become part of the growing interest group community in Washington (Donato 1990) and are making significant headway in all areas of lobbying. Over the last few decades, the number of corporations with Washington offices has skyrocketed and, along with this, the number of corporate government relations officials. Women's increased involvement in corporate lobbying contributes significantly to this growth. Although it was just a short time ago that corporations were looked down on for sending a woman to do their business on the Hill, women have now established themselves as legitimate players in the business–government nexus.

But it has not been without a fight. In the early 1980s, along with increasing numbers of women in government, women began to enter positions as government relations representatives for major corporations in Washington. Initially, women in these positions were not taken very seriously by those in business or government. Unlike their female counterparts on the Hill—women staffers who were already involved in writing key pieces of legislation—corporate women "downtown" were, according to one of my interviewees, "still serving coffee." Moreover, women corporate lobbyists were excluded from the male-dominated networks where important information and knowledge is shared and a common culture established; thus, they lacked crucial resources needed to do their jobs. As women became increasingly frustrated with their exclusion from old boys networks, they decided to take action. A small group of women lobbyists for major corporations in Washington took it upon themselves to form a "women's network," where they could obtain and share information and career advice through informal and formal events and activities and through organizational membership. These early corporate lobbyists took it upon themselves to be vigilant in mentoring younger women in the field and pushing corporate heads to hire more women in the area of government relations. Their hard work paid off. Several younger women interviewed for this book claim that, had it not been for the efforts of these pioneering women, they probably wouldn't be in the field.

The women I encountered through the various phases of my research for this book, without exception, said that working as a government relations official is a "good job for women." Compared with other occupations where women are concentrated, even compared with most other managerial jobs, corporate government relations officials earn high salaries and have high visibility. There are also opportunities for advancement within corporate government relations operations. A couple of decades ago only a handful of women were at the top of the government relations hierarchy. By 1995, a quarter of all Washington offices were headed by women. Half of all government relations "managers" are were women.

Still, it appears that, among corporate government relations officials for major U.S. corporations, there is almost no diversity by race and ethnicity. This may be partly due to the fact that staffers with whom they interact are mostly white, which may influence corporate hiring decisions. Also, black women are underrepresented in prestigious law schools where women prepare to enter the field of corporate government relations. None of my interviewees for this book were black women or other women of color. At the Tax Alliance retreat, only one of the attendees was non-white. I accompanied this woman for breakfast one morning, where she spoke briefly of her experiences as the only non-white woman in the organization. As a woman in a male-dominated field, and a woman of color in a predominantly white organization, she reported that at first she was a bit uncomfortable, but that the other women have been very supportive and welcoming. She looked forward to increased racial-ethnic diversity among the Tax Alliance members in the future because, as she said, that would make it "easier" for new women to assimilate into the organization.

For women who have made their way into the field of corporate lobbying, there has been a significant amount of advancement with regard to their integration into the Washington lobbying scene. Just as men in the field have done for a very long time, women have begun to incorporate themselves into activities, events, and formal organizations where they can establish and nurture relationships with legislators, staffers, and government relations officials from other companies. They are increasingly pushing for inclusion into formerly male "clubs," restaurants, and other social spheres. The Burning Tree golf course, once a bastion of elite male networking, is now open to women members. Women continue to work hard toward inclusion because they know it is in these environments where important information is share and access obtained. In a major battle over the inclusion of women as members of the elite Augusta National Club, Martha Burk, chair of the National Council of Women's Organizations (NCWO), says, "Far from being a place where friends gather for golf, Augusta National is a gathering of corporate power players like no other. Deals are made, careers are changed, and even national policy is affected through relationships such as those of the nineteen members of Augusta National who sit on the Council on Foreign Relations. All of this while shutting women out." According to Burk (National Council of Women's Organizations [NCWO] 2005), there are 1,000 corporations and other institutions with direct links to Augusta.

Although women lobbyists are increasingly penetrating the old boys network in Washington, D.C., they are still "outsiders" in many ways. Even when women are admitted into the "club," they are not always treated equally or fully integrated. Thus, women are beginning to form their own networking associations, such as the Women's Congressional Golf Association (WCGA), a group of over 200 women lobbyists and staffers who learn how to play golf and, at the same time, learn what is going on in business and government. The last couple of decades have also seen a substantial increase in professional and policy organizations in Washington that bring women in government affairs together, such as the Secure Retirement Coalition, Women in Government Relations, and the Tax Alliance.

According to several of the members, the Tax Alliance (examined in chapter 4) "broke the mold" among women's organizations in that it has become a highly respected and effective policy discussion group consisting of corporate lobbyists well as government officials. So well respected, in fact, that, according to several members, "men would love to be part of it." The Tax Alliance women have regular meetings in Washington where they invite legislative staffers, legislators, and officials from government agencies like the IRS and Treasury to speak about what is happening on the Hill regarding tax policy and other related issues. Like other policy organizations, they hold annual retreats at secluded luxury resorts where they can relax, play sports, soak in the spa, and hold formal sessions. The annual retreat provides women lobbyists with important career and policy information as well as access to those who participate in writing tax legislation. Moreover, the interactions, activities, and rituals that take place at meetings and retreats serve to solidify a common bond among the members and maintain the concept of a business-government "tax family."

My research finds that, although both men and women lobbyists actively network with key people in business and government in and out of organizational contexts, women are less likely than men to interact with those at the top levels, specifically legislators and corporate heads. However, women corporate lobbyists are significantly more likely than men to interact in various ways with those at similar levels, namely lobbyists at other corporations or trade associations and legislative staff. My research also finds that women lobbyists are significantly more likely than their male counterparts to network with other women lobbyists and women staffers. More specifically, they are more likely to talk on the phone, share a meal, and "socialize" (e.g., attend a concert or sporting event) with other women in business and government.

Researchers have argued that women should form heterogeneous ties if the expect to gain power and influence. Some claim that "encouraging women to form networks with other women may be unnecessary, or at worst nonproductive" (Brass 1985, 340, 341 in Scott 1996). Social scientists generally agree that ties with those at the top (usually men) are most useful (Brass 1985; Kanter 1977). It is admittedly the case that ties with those at the top of organizations may provide women with access to key information they may not be able to obtain from those at similar levels, since these are the people who set policy. However, within the context of corporate-government relations, women's ties with other women and men at similar levels in government are not insignificant. As argued in previous chapters, they may be equally, if not more, instrumental in shaping policy as ties with those at the top. Legislative staffers know the technical details that make them essential in writing and interpreting legislation and preparing the way for communication with the legislator or committee chair. As one corporate lobbyist told me, "It matters that you don't be seen as jumping over staff, but need to bring them into whatever relationship you have with the elected official. Because they rely on their staffs entirely. I mean there are a handful of legislators who know the nitty-gritty details of how something gets developed and works through the process, but very few—they rely entirely on staff." And now that women staffers and corporate lobbyists have been around long enough to have experience working on not just one, but two or three versions of a particular piece of legislation (e.g., the tax code), ties with women in other corporations and on legislative staffs are more important than ever in the process.

CREDIBILITY AND HEGEMONIC MASCULINITY

For almost all of the women who participated in this study, what is most important in achieving access and influence, and thus success in the field, is that they are viewed as "credible," taken "seriously" as key players in the corporate-government relationship. Women lobbyists interviewed for the book repeatedly spoke of how they have finally achieved credibility in Washington. But it wasn't easy, and they have to work hard every day to hold onto it. As tokens in a sea of male corporate lobbyists until just recently, women have had to struggle to be viewed as credible. Several of the corporate women who founded the Tax Alliance, now in their late fifties, spoke of how they "paved the way" for younger generations in this regard. Says one, "We are sort of the vanguard, my generation. And so we have had to push harder to get that credibility. To be recognized for what we can do in this job. Hopefully it is going to be easier for the younger generations. But, at some point, you have got to pay the price."

Although the women do not recognize it as such, the "price" they pay includes that of reproducing hegemonic masculinity. Hegemonic masculinity is embedded in practices and policy that instills and maintains privilege (Connell and Messerschmidt 2005). When women work to portray themselves and their organizations as credible, they are in effect adapting to a masculinist structure and culture (Martin 2003) that attributes certain ways of interacting, activities, and policy areas that are associated with men and the public sphere as instrumental and important—and hence credible. This can be seen in how the women interviewed characterize issue areas commonly associated with men and masculinity as important, and those associated with women and femininity as relatively unimportant. For instance, when the women in this study speak of their work and their organizations, they go to great lengths to emphasize that they do not focus on women's rights, but on "serious issues" such as tax policy. As one of the founders of the Tax Alliance says, regarding the group's success at "breaking the mold" and achieving credibility in Washington, "It wasn't a women's rights type of thing or anything of the sort. We didn't deal with women's issues. We dealt with tax issues, you know, issues that were important, and I think that's what helps make it more credible in a way, or just trying to break away from that." In fact, one of the reasons women have entered the realm of tax policy, defense, and other "male" policy areas is because they see these as a more serious areas than, for example, health care or family policy—areas viewed as associated with women's issues.

Women maintain and reinforce hegemonic masculinity not only by leaving unchallenged the idea that issues characterized as masculine are more important than those characterized as feminine, but also by claiming that public policy is gender-neutral. For example, tax policy contributes to gender inequality in both material and ideological ways. The current tax system discourages women from working outside the home. Moreover, by considering (in most cases) women as "secondary" earners, it reinforces traditional gender ideologies that position women as primary caregivers and men as primary breadwinners. Current tax policy also contributes to women's poverty because it discourages marriage among poor women. Thus, tax policy is very much a woman's issue. Yet the women lobbyists and staffers interviewed for this book insist that tax policy is not a "gender thing. The issues do not separate on gender."

Another way women lobbyists reinforce hegemonic masculinity is by characterizing and emphasizing masculinized[1] activities and events that they engage in at their meetings and retreats as productive and instrumental relative to feminized activities and events. In their attempt to gain credibility with their bosses and the larger Washington community, the Tax Alliance women stress the "serious," "productive" activities that go on at their retreat. They emphasize the formal sessions held each morning where corporate government relations managers, legislative staff, and agency officials give speeches concerning the federal budget, tax shelters, and the social security program. They mention the ten-pound binders that weigh them down over the course of the meeting but that also serve to send the message that what they are doing is, to use the words of the Tax Alliance women, "substantive" and "weighty." And they may talk about the round or two of golf they played with a staffer who works for someone on the House Ways and Means Committee or a Treasury official.

In contrast, women downplay the instrumentality of the networking that takes place while they soak in mineral waters or have facials, or engage in any other activities that might be characterized as "frivolous." In order to gain credibility on the "outside," women work hard to downplay feminized activities, such as soaking in the spa, shopping, talking about childcare, which are not viewed as instrumental and productive, but rather expressive and unproductive. At the same time, it is apparent that women recognize and use the femininized character of their activities and interactions when they argue that they form closer bonds with those in government while they are in the spa than men could ever hope to form on the golf course. The women describe their networks and organizations as providing a "safe" environment in which to share information and form bonds. Relative to mixed-gender contexts, women describe an environment that is non-competitive, supportive, and nurturing; where they receive acknowledgement and reward for being strong and assertive women. Unlike masculinist mixed-gender policy groups and retreats (like the Tax Council) and larger organizations for which they work, where there is a "valorization of men and masculinities over women and femininities" (Martin 1996, 192), there are no significant costs in doing femininity within the boundaries of all-women networks and organizations.

There are, however, some hidden costs embedded in adapting to a wider masculinist structure and culture in public, while valorizing women and femininities in private. By acting as though tax policy is not a woman's issues, and reserving "doing femininity" for behind closed doors at all-women retreats or other social occasions, hegemonic masculinity is maintained and, along with it, male privilege. This has negative consequences for women lobbyists and women as a whole. For example, downplaying or hiding the instrumentality and importance of activities and interactions characterized as female disadvantages women in their attempt to balance work and family responsibilities. Like the "feminized" aspects of government affairs work, family work is characterized in ways that correspond with what it means to be a woman and femininity, and therefore remains unrecognized and unrewarded compared to other forms of work. Women corporate lobbyists work in highly demanding jobs. My research shows that women put in as many hours as their male colleagues at work. Moreover, corporate lobbying often require attendance at evening fundraisers and other events that can interfere with family time. Yet women report spending three times as many hours on housework and childcare as men. They are also more likely than men to have small children at home. By leaving un-challenged masculine structures and policies at work, and there-fore reinforcing hegemonic masculinity, women lobbyists are not doing themselves any favors at home.

There are substantial incentives in our society for women (and men) to turn their backs on the structures and mechanisms that reinforce gender inequality. Those who adapt to masculinist structures and organizations are likely to be viewed as compe-tent and credible, and rewarded as such. It is much less reward-ing, and often much more risky, to engage in struggles related to women's interests. One especially candid legislative aide inter-viewed for this book said that when representatives of women's groups visit her legislator to present their cases, they are often perceived as representing "guerilla"[2] groups and their perspec-tives viewed as "radical." They are not seen as credible. In fact, they are often not seen at all. They certainly don't have the op-portunity to soak in the spa with legislators and their staffs. For those who adapt to, and struggle for, systems and structures that support the dominant groups, by class, race, gender, or sexuality, there are significant rewards.

THE BEST-KEPT SECRETS

For all the advancements women have made in the realm of corporate lobbying, they don't get much attention from schol-ars, political pundits, or the media. Compared with mixed-gender policy organizations and discussions groups, like the Business Council and the Tax Council, and all-male social clubs like the Bohemian Grove, the networks formed by women lob-byists have been relatively invisible. This is partly because those at the top of the formal power structure are the ones who typi-cally get the most attention, both positive and negative. In their second-tier positions within organizations, women government relations officials and staffers are not considered as important or influential, and thus not as newsworthy, as those at the top. But

it is also because the women themselves would rather attention
be diverted from networks and organizations where they can
"safely" do gender away from the scrutiny of men. Moreover,
in their attempt to be seen as credible, women work hard to
become fully integrated into the lobbying scene in Washington,
and therefore do not want to attract unusual attention for sepa-
rating themselves out as women.

That women corporate lobbyists tend not to be in the
spotlight is precisely what makes them so effective in strengthening business-government relations and hence business power
in the political realm. Particularly at this moment in history,
when corporations and legislators are under increased scrutiny for their dubious actions, it is especially important that
they not be seen as doing anything unethical or illegal. High-
powered lobbyists, like Jack Abramoff, who for years wined
and dined legislators and legislative aides in "his restaurants and
skyboxes and jetted off with them to Scotland and the Pacific
Island of Saipan," and in the process shaped policy, are in a
heap of trouble (Schmidt and Grimaldi 2005). Now, more than
ever, corporations and government officials want attention diverted away from their connections and the mechanisms used
to maintain and strengthen them. This makes the relatively invisible networks and organizations of women lobbyists especially useful. While women corporate government relations officials are meeting in secluded locations where they relax, have
facials, and play golf with aides to legislators who serve on the
Ways and Means and Senate Finance Committee and IRS and
Treasury officials, while they are learning how to shoot with
other women lobbyists who work for Jack Abramoff's best
friends[3]—all the while sharing important policy information
and obtain access and influence—the focus is on the actions
and interactions of men at the top. In some ways, this may leave
them even more room and freedom to exert influence than
they would otherwise have.

On top of this, the feminized character of women's interactions and organizations creates an environment that is ideal
for forming and maintaining strong business–government ties.
Whether women's and men's interactions and activities and retreats actually differ is beyond the scope of this analysis and,
in some ways, misses the point. As chapter 4 argues, more important is that women (and men) characterize women's actions
and interactions, particularly with other women, as different
than those of men. The women lobbyists and staffers included in
this study characterize their bonds as closer, more intimate than
those of men, particularly those at the top of business and government. As one of my interviewees said, she couldn't imagine
that men create the same "long-lasting bonds and friendships"
at golf tournaments as the women do at their retreats. The Tax
Alliance women describe their activities, such as the bowling
tournament, as non-competitive compared with men's. As "evidence," the women point out that at the Sequins Only banquet,
a "Worst Bowler" award is presented. The tournament is not
really a competition, they say, but a chance to be humiliated in a
relaxed and supportive environment.

Repeatedly, the women lobbyists and staffers I spoke with
stressed the support they provide each other in the form of career and policy information. They describe their interactions not
as lobbying but as "teaching" and "learning." Legislative staff are
particularly eager to learn from corporate-government relations
officials who typically have more experience. Many corporate-
government relations officials began as legislative aides. Moving
"downtown" from the Hill is considered a big step up because
corporate-government relations jobs are better paying, provide
better "perks," and come with greater prestige. This career trajectory greatly advantages corporations in several ways. First, it
creates a dependency relationship in which legislative aides need
the support and mentorship of women corporate-government
relations officials if they hope to move up in their careers. By

forming close alliances, they are assured of that support. Second, as former colleagues and friends, corporate women who worked on the Hill would be expected to have greater access to legislators and staffers. My research finds, in fact, that women corporate-government relations officials who previously worked for a legislator (staffer) are significantly more likely than those who did not to interact with both legislators and staffers in a variety of contexts (talking on the phone, sharing meals, attending social events). Third, women who previously worked on the Hill enter corporations with "insider" information about what is happening in government.

Gendered characterizations of women lobbyists' activities and interactions, the nature of their career paths, and the lack of public attention to their interactions and organizations, contribute to business' advantaged position vis-à-vis gaining information and access in the political realm. Women lobbyists are in an ideal position to establish strong relationships with those in government and enhance business power. Women say that they feel "safe" and "secure" in their interactions with other women at meetings and retreats. Several women described the Tax Alliance as "safe haven" where women can engage in interaction, activities, and events free of the oppression and ostracism they feel in mixed-gender and male-dominated contexts. It makes sense that if women characterize their interactions and activities in "feminized" ways, as non-competitive, nurturing, comforting, and supportive (rather than instrumental and productive), then they are likely to feel "closer" to and "safer." In addition, staffers are likely to want to form especially close bonds with corporate women on whom they are dependent for career advancement. Together with this, if women lobbyists and staffers feel that, relative to men's ties, their bonds are safer, closer, and more secure, they may not be as guarded in their sharing of policy information.

At the same time, women work very hard at doing and mobilizing masculinity in order to be taken seriously. When I remarked on the extremely high caliber of the women I encountered in the course of my study, an interviewee responded, "There are some very, very good people. But, see, you know the difference is for us to get to where we are, we have to be better than men doing the same thing. That's all there is to it . . . I mean you really have to be better and you have to prove you are better. So if you're not as good as some of these women are, you wouldn't get to where you are." As one corporate lobbyist put it, "you've got to play their games." Compared to the past, when many women entered corporate-government relations jobs from teaching careers, they now tend to enter the field after educations at prestigious law schools, where they increasingly specialize in "male" policy areas such as taxes. They work very hard to become highly expert in their fields so they will be effective in their jobs and so they will be viewed as "serious" players in the business-government nexus. At their meetings and through their interactions and activities, they mobilize masculinity by holding formal sessions and distributing huge amounts of materials. In various ways, they work hard not to be viewed as frivolous women, but as serious corporate political professionals.

Women's entrance into corporate lobbying is good for business-government relations and business power. Women lobbyists do and mobilize both masculinity and femininity in ways that create and maintain trusting, open, and strong relations with those in government, and at the same time produce a cadre of highly trained, highly expert women corporate officials who work hard to be seen as credible in the political arena. They use their connections and expertise to help corporations save and make billions of dollars each year.

It is nearly impossible to measure precisely to what extent, and how, women (or men) lobbyists' connections with those in government influence policy for at least a couple of significant reasons. First, much of the influence exerted by powerful organizations on the legislative process, and decisions made as a result, happen behind closed doors, away from public view. Reporters and other "outsiders" are generally not permitted entry into the meetings and retreats of the economic and political elite. Second, corporations often benefit most when certain pieces of legislation, or the particular wording of legislation, are never introduced. As one corporate lobbyist says, a large part of her job consists of making sure "nothing happens" legislatively: "I describe my job as a legislative oncologist because most of the time I am trying to prevent things from happening."

The relative invisibility of women's organizations and networks and their effects on policy make women lobbyists one of the best-kept secrets corporations have in maintaining business hegemony and business power. This book argues that women's secluded and exclusive networks and activities are instrumental in shaping policy to the advantage of business. They help maintain corporate hegemony by supporting policy that diverts resources away from those on the bottom and redistributes them to those at the top. At the same time, hegemonic masculinity is reinforced through corporate-supported policy that continues to reflect and reproduce a masculinist structure where men and masculinity are "valorized" and women and femininity are devalued or go unrecognized. As long as the focus is on those at the top of business and government, and as long as dominant gender ideologies portray women's actions and interactions as less important and instrumental than those of men, attention will be diverted away from women lobbyists and staffers who meet behind closed doors, attend teas, soak in hot tubs, and shape policy that serves to benefit business and the elite but disadvantage everyone else.

We are living in a political-economic era when corporations continue to gain wealth and power in the United States and around the world. Corporate executive salaries continue to soar while those at the bottom are doing worse every day. The top fifth of all income earners in the United States earn half of all the income in the country, up from 44 percent two decades ago. With regard to wealth, the gap is even greater, with the top fifth owning and controlling 84 percent of wealth in the United States, while the bottom 60 percent own and control a measly 5 percent. The bottom fifth actually have "negative wealth," meaning that they are in debt (U.S. Bureau of the Census 2004). And more and more people are finding themselves in that position every day. Putting money into savings, investment, or retirement isn't a even a consideration when people are struggling to survive on a day-to-day basis. Because of persistent gender ideologies and gendered public policy, women, particularly those who head households, suffer most.

At the same time, faced with foreign competition, corporations' use various mechanisms to ensure that their wealth and power is protected. They downsize their U.S. operations and shift production and labor to foreign countries or to certain areas of the United States, where labor is cheap and governmental regulations are weak, in an effort to increase profit (Perucci and Wysong 1999). In a current "flexible" global capitalist economy, where worldwide access to production, consumer, and labor markets is increasing, corporations and corporate heads have enormous potential to increase their economic and political power, while workers become increasingly vulnerable. In Bangladesh and Honduras, and elsewhere in the world, corporations like Nike and Gap employ people, a high proportion of whom are women and children, to work long hours in substandard conditions where they are often paid below the minimum wage. Unionization efforts are often met with threats of firing or moving production to another country where there is more available labor and less resistance, hence the looming China threat.

Sweatshops are not confined to foreign countries; they exist right here in the United States. Los Angeles is currently considered the garment manufacturing center of the United States. Many companies have relocated from other areas of the country to L.A. in recent years. Because numerous small subcontractors can be used for production, most of which operate with little oversight, and because garment workers are mostly immigrant women who are willing to work for less and are less likely to resist exploitation, L.A. is extremely attractive to corporations in the garment industry. As Bonacich and Appelbaum (2006, 297) state, "L.A. can indeed be described as the 'sweatshop capital of the United States.'"

In a global economy, it has become more important than ever for corporations to maintain vigilance in areas such as tax, environmental, and labor policy. In the past several decades, corporations have rallied to maintain and increase their power in the political realm to protect their economic interests in this country and around the world. They have put enormous, and unequalled, resources into building up their government relations operations in Washington and elsewhere in the country, and hiring top-notch lawyers and outside consultants, many of whom with prior careers in government. Now, more than ever, it is crucial that we pay attention to the mechanisms and processes used by corporations to reinforce business-government relations and maintain business power. More specifically, and generally neglected so far in the literature, we need to pay closer attention to the dynamics of class, race, gender, ethnicity, and sexuality, as they affect, and are affected by, business-government relations.

Gender and family ideologies are in flux. An increasing number of women are entering the political arena at all levels—as lobbyists, legislators, legislative aides, counsels to key legislative committees, government regulatory and agency officials, and, perhaps very soon, as president of the country. It is time that social and political scientists and pundits devote more attention to women's movement into these positions, and gender, as they interact with public policy, business interests, and the interests of women as a whole in the United States. It is my hope that this book provides a start.

NOTES

CHAPTER 1 INTRODUCTION AND OVERVIEW

1. "Doing gender" refers to the ongoing production and reproduction of masculinity and femininity through daily activities, interactions, and events. To "use" or "mobilize" gender is to enact masculinity (or masculinities) and femininity within various contexts to achieve desired ends (Lorber 1989; Martin 2003, 2001, 1996). For instance, Martin (1996) notes that when women mobilize competitive masculinity at work in order to get ahead, men may view their enactments as illegitimate or unattractive.

CHAPTER 2 FROM PRIVATE TO PUBLIC INTERESTS

1. Nancy Cott (1977) notes that (elite) women's writings were used in ministers' sermons as well as by educators and authors.
2. The Heritage Foundation, a Washington conservative think tank, is comprised of "experts" in particular areas of public policy. Most of the foundation members are corporate officials and academics who specialize in areas of national defense, tax, and social security policy.
3. "K Street" is Washington insiders' shorthand for Washington's lawyer-lobbyist complex.
4. Organizational data were obtained from the 1980, 1986, and 1995 editions of *Washington Representatives.*

CHAPTER 3 THE PROBLEM WITH NO NAME?

1. The National Committee to Preserve Social Security and Medicare is a grassroots organization representing 5.5 million seniors. The report referred to here uses data from the well-respected Employee Benefit Research Institute.
2. The "family wage" was instituted in the early 1900s by manufacturing companies. In theory, a family wage paid the head of household (a man) a wage enough to support the entire family.

3. Blum and Stracuzzi (2004), for example, refer to Prozac and its "chemical cousins as the new "mother's little helpers." I would argue that the wide use of anti-depressants among women is linked to the gendered nature of "hyperparenting" in the United States.

4. Ralph Nader came on the scene with the publication of *Unsafe at Any Speed* in 1965, and led a consumer campaign for the federal regulation of auto safety (Clawson, Neustadtl, and Scott 1992).

5. See Clawson, Neustadtl, and Scott 1992; Mintz 2002; Mintz and Schwartz 1985; Prechel 2000, 2003; Schwartz 1987.

Chapter 4   Warm Springs and Hot Topics at the Tax Alliance Retreat

1. Several women spoke casually during dinner about "sharing" or "building" knowledge through interaction at the retreat.

2. One legislative aide informed me that public- and private-sector representatives mostly serve on the Tax Alliance Membership Commission and the Entertainment Commission.

3. She is described as a "very close friend" who is very committed to remaining "part of the group." According to one Tax Alliance woman, she "cares for the group and respects it a great deal. She gave up a trip to a nephew's birthday party who she is very, very close with, that she apparently never missed before, in order to come to the retreat this year."

4. Because of my "outsider" status, I did not understand many of the jokes and suggestive comments.

5. After a game of golf, one can always enjoy a spa treatment called Golfers Glow "to eliminate a few rough spots" or "if your goal is reducing wrinkles."

6. I was not able to gather systematic data on the number of children in attendance. Most of the children present at the retreat attended a daycare facility, so I did not have much opportunity to interact with them. I learned of their presence mostly through conversations with the retreat participants. I did pay a visit to the daycare center (which actually provides care in the evening as well), which is located in a colorful, cheery, sterile building on the periphery of the hotel grounds. The center is run by a staff of professionals and offers a variety of structured activities for the children, including classes in ceramics, painting, and sports.

7. When a husband or partner was present at the dinner table where I sat, in all but one case he was placed next to me. When I mentioned this to the women I interviewed following the retreat, they wrote it off as purely coincidental.

8. According on woman I interviewed, some men refer to the Tax Alliance women as the "tax chicks."

CHAPTER 5 THE COSTS AND BENEFITS OF FAMILY TIES

1. Manke et al. (1994) finds fathers, regardless of income status, to increase household participation on the weekends. Employed women's participation in household work also increases on the weekends. The opposite is the case for women in single-earner households; their participation decreases on the weekends.

2. As reported by survey respondents, the range for women in government affairs is from twenty to seventy hours per week, the range for men is from five to seventy hours per week. The top 25 percent of men report working seventy hours per week in their government relations job, the top 25 percent of women report working anywhere from sixty-five to seventy hours per week.

CHAPTER 6 WOMEN, CORPORATE LOBBYING, AND POWER

1. The terms "masculinized" and "feminized" refer to behaviors, activities, events, and organizations that are characterized in ways that correspond with characterizations of men and masculinity and women and femininity, respectively.

2. Guerilla is a term used to describe groups or tactics that are typically aggressive in nature. Sometimes these tactics involve the use of violence, but the primary purpose of guerilla groups is typically to disrupt the normal state of affairs. Some groups that struggle for women's interests identify themselves as "guerilla groups," but typically use the term in sarcastic or humorous ways to attract attention to issues of gender inequality. On their Web site, the Guerilla Girls, a well-known theatrical touring group, say that they "use humor to convey information, provoke discussion, and show that feminists can be funny. We wear gorilla masks to focus on the issues rather than our personalities."

3. Grover Norquist, who is a close friend of Abramoff, heads the Americans for Tax Reform, is also on the National Rifle Association board. He is also the boss of Megan McChesney, who shoots at orange saucers with other lobbyists and legislative staff.

References

Ackley, K. 2005. "It's Tee Time for Women Lobbyists." Women's Congressional Golf Association. *Section News,* August 8:1–2, www.wcga.org.

Aldrich, H. and P. R. Reese. 1994. "Gender Gap, Gender Myth: Does Women's Networking Behavior Differ Significantly From Men's?" Paper presented at the Global Conference on Entrepreneurship, INSEAD.

Alexander, A. 2000. "The Tax Policy Regime in American Politics, 1941–1951." *Congress and the Presidency.* 27:59–80.

Allen, Mike. 2005. "House GOP Weighs Preapproval of Sponsored Travel." *The Washington Post.* May 11:A5.

Archibald, George. 2002. "Feminists Lobby for U.N. Rights Pact." *The Washington Times.* May 28:A1.

Barlett, L .D. and J. B. Steele. 1998. "Corporate Welfare." *Time.* November, 9:1–4, www.time.com/time/magazine.

Bath, M. G., J. Gayvert-Owen, A. Nownes. 2005. "Women Lobbyists: The Gender Gap and Interest Representation. *Politics and Policy.* 33:136–151.

Bianchi, S., M. Milkie, L. Sayer, J. Robinson. 2000. "Is Anyone Doing the Housework? Trends in the Gender Division of Household Labor." *Social Forces.* 79(1):121–228.

Birnbaum, Jeffrey. 2005. "2nd Senator to Return Abramoff Funds: Lobbyist Paid Columnist. *The Washington Post.* December 17:A2.

Birnbaum, Jeffrey. 2006. "Women, Minorities Make Up New Generation of Lobbyists." *The Washington Post.* May 1:D1.

Blum, L. and N. Stracuzzi. 2004. "Gender in the Prozac Nation: Popular Discourse and Productive Femininity." *Gender & Society.* 18:269–286.

Blum L. and V. Smith. 1988. "Women's Mobility in the Corporation: A Critique of the Politics of Optimism." *Signs.* 13:528–545.

Bodfield, Rhonda. 2002. "Women Flex Lobbying Muscles." *The Arizona Daily Star.* February 9:A4.

Bonacich, Edna and R. P. Appelbaum. 2006. "Behind the Label: The Return of the Sweatshop." In *Working in America,* 284–298, edited by Amy Wharton. New York: McGraw Hill.

148 References

Bookman, A. and S. Morgen. 1988. *Women and the Politics of Empowerment*. Philadelphia: Temple University Press.

Borger, Julian. 2005. "Growing Corruption Scandal Threatens to Engulf Republicans." *The Guardian*. November 23:15.

Bourdieu, Pierre. 1984. *Distinction: A Social Critique of the Judgment of Taste*. Cambridge: Harvard University Press.

Brass, D. 1985. "Men's and Women's Networks: A Study of Interaction Patterns and Influence in an Organization." *Academy of Management Journal*. 23:327–343.

Brass, D. 1992. "Power in Organizations: A Social Network Perspective." In *Research in Politics and Society*, 295–323, edited by Alan Whitt and Gwen Moore. Greenwich: JAI Press.

Broder, John. 2006. "Amid Scandals, State Overhaul Lobbying Laws." *The New York Times*. January 24:A1.

Cancian, F. 1986. "The Feminization of Love." *Signs*. 11:692–709.

Carr-Elsing, D. 1999. "Women of Influence: Lobbyists Use Negotiation Skills." *The Capital Times* (Madison, WI). September 30:1F.

The Center for Public Integrity. 2003. "How the Feds Stack Up." May 15. http://www.publicintegrity.org/hiredguns.

Citizens for Tax Justice. 2002a. "Corporate Freeloader Chief is Bush's Choice to Head Treasury." December 9:1.

Citizens for Tax Justice. 2002b. "Surge in Corporate Tax Welfare Drives Corporate Tax Payments Down to Near Record Low." April 17:1–4.

Citizens for Tax Justice. 2003a. "More Corporate Tax Shelters on the Way?" October 14:1–3.

Citizens for Tax Justice. 2003b. "Testimony of Robert S. McIntyre, Director, Citizens for Tax Justice, Before the Committtee on the Budget, United States House of Representatives," June 18.

Citizens for Tax Justice. 2005. "House Energy Bill Rewards Corporate Tax Avoiders." April 21:1–2.

Clawson, D., A. Neustadtl, D. Scott. 1992. *Money Talks: Corporate PACs and Political Influence*. New York: Basic Books.

Collins, S. 1997. *Black Corporate Executives: The Making and Braking of a Black Middle Class*. Philadelphia: Temple University Press.

Connell, R. W. 1995. *Masculinities*. Berkeley: University of California Press

Connell, R. W. and J. Messerschmidt. 2005. "Hegemonic Masculinity: Rethinking the Concept." *Gender & Society*. 19:829–859.

Cott, N. F. 1977. *The Bonds of Womanhood: "Women's Sphere" in New England, 1980–1835*. New Haven: Yale University Press.

Coverman, S. 1989. "Women's Work Is Never Done: The Division of Domestic Labor." In *Women: A Feminist Perspective*, 356–368, edited by Jo Freeman. Fourth edition. Palo Alto: Mayfield Publishing Co.

Crittendon, A. 2001. *The Price of Motherhood: Why the Most Important Job in the World is Still the Least Valued.* New York: Henry Holt and Company.

Cusak, B. J. Dufour, G. E., J. Hearn, J. Kaplan, M. Scully, J. Snyder, J. Young. 2005. "Top Lobbyists—Hired Guns." *The Hill.* April 27:1–6.

diLeonardo, M. 1987. "The Female World of Cards and Holidays: Women, Families, and the Work of Kinship." *Signs.* 12:440–453.

Domhoff, G. W. 1974. *The Bohemian Grove and Other Retreats.* New York: Harper Collins.

Domhoff, G. W. 2001. *Who Rules America? Power and Politics.* Fourth Edition. New York: McGraw Hill.

Donato, K. M. 1990. "Keepers of the Corporate Image." In *Job Queues, Gender Queues: Explaining Women's Inroads Into Male Occupations,* 129–143, edited by Barbara Reskin and Patricia Roos. Philadelphia: Temple University Press.

Dublin, T. 1994. *Transforming Women's Work: New England Lives in the Industrial Revolution.* Ithaca, NY: Cornell University Press.

Economist, The. 2006. "Hobbling the Lobbyists: Pork and Scandals." January 28:29.

Edin, K. and L. Lein. 1997. *Making Ends Meet: How Single Mothers Survive Welfare and Low-Wage Work.* New York: Russell Sage Foundation.

Ferree, M. M. 1991. "The Gender Division of Labor in Two-Earner Marriages. *Journal of Family Issues.* 12:158–180.

Folbre, N. 2001. *The Invisible Heart: Economics and Family Values.* New York: The New Press.

Folbre, N. 1993. "Micro, Macro, Choice, and Structure." In *Theory on Gender, Feminism on Theory,* 323–330, edited by P. England. New York: Aldine de Gruyter.

Francis, D. 1999. "Bye-bye Corporate Tax Revenues." Opinion Column. *Christian Science Monitor.* November 3:1–4. www.csmonitor.com.

Galloway, Jim. 2006a. "Reed, Abramoff Flew For $92,000: Cost of Private Jet Revealed." *The Atlanta Journal.* May 27:E3.

Galloway, Jim. 2006b. "Tribes Filtered $5 Million to Reed, Report Concludes." *The Atlanta Journal—Constitution.* June 23:E1.

Gerstel, N. and S. Gallagher. 1994. "Caring For Kith and Kin: Gender, Employment, and the Privatization of Care." *Social Problems.* 41:519–539.

Gerstel, N. and H. E. Gross. 1989. "Women and the American family: Continuity and Change." In *Women: A Feminist Perspective,* 89–120, edited by Jo Freeman. Fourth edition. Palo Alto: Mayfield Publishing Co.

Ghiloni, B. W. 1987. "The Velvet Ghetto: Women, Power, and the Corporation." In *Power Elites and Organizations,* 21–36, edited by G. William Domhoff and Thomas R. Dye. Beverly Hills: Sage Publications.

Gilligan, Carol. 1982. *In a Different Voice: Psychological Theory and Women's Development.* Cambridge: Harvard University Press.

Gramsci, Antonio. 1972. *Selections from "The Prison Notebooks of Antonio Gramsci."* Edited and translated by Quintin Hoare and G. Nowell Smith. New York: International Publishers.

Granovetter, M. 1973. "The Strength of Weak Ties." *American Journal of Sociology.* 78:1360–1380.

Hanchard, M. 1996. "Cultural Politics and Black Public Intellectuals." *Social Text.* 48:95–108.

Hartmann, H. 1979. "The Unhappy Marriage of Marxism and Feminism." *Capital and Class.* Summer (8):1–3.

Hartmann, H. and R. Spalter-Roth. 1996. "A Feminist Approach to Public Policy Making for Women and Families. *Current Persepctives in Social Theory.* 16:33–51.

Hartsock, N. 1983. *Money, Sex, and Power: Toward a Historical Materialism.* Boston: Northeastern University Press.

Hartsock, N. 1989. "Foucault on Power: A Theory for Women?" In *Feminism/Postmodernism,* 157–175, edited by Linda Nicholson. New York: Routledge.

Heberle, R. 1999. "Disciplining Gender: Or, Are Women Getting Away with Murder?" *Signs.* 24:4.

Hertz, R. 1986. *More Equal Than Others: Women and Men in Dual-Career Marriages.* Berkeley: University of California Press.

Hill, C. 2000. "Privatizing Social Security is Bad, Particularly for Women." *Dollars & Sense.* November:17.

Hochschild, A. R. 1983. *The Managed Heart: Commercialization of Human Feeling.* Berkeley: University of California Press.

Hochschild, A. R. 1989. *The Second Shift.* New York: Viking.

Hurt, Charles. 2003. "Feminists Criticize Female Court Picks." *The Washington Times.* April 28:A5.

Hurt, Charles and Ralph Hallow. 2005. "Women's Group Calls for Miers Withdrawal." *The Washington Times.* October 27:A1.

Institute for Policy Studies. 2001. "New CEO/Worker Pay Gap Study." From the Institute for Policy Studies and United for a Fair Economy report, "Executive Excess 2001: Layoffs, Tax Rebates and the Gender Gap, Institute for Policy Studies."

Institute for Women's Policy Research. 2000. "Why Privatizing Social Security Would Hurt Women." *Research-in-Brief.* March:1–6.

Institute on Taxation and Economic Policy. 2000. "Study Finds Resurgence in Corporate Tax Avoidance." October 19:1–4.

Jacobs, J. 1995. "Trends in Earnings, Authority, and Values Among Salaried Managers." In *Gender Inequality at Work,* 152–177, edited by J. Jacobs. Thousand Oaks, CA: Sage.

Johnston, D. K. 2006. "A Boon for the Richest In an Estate Tax Repeal." *The New York Times.* June 7:pC8(L).

Johnston, D. K. 2000. "Corporate Taxes Fall, But Citizens Are Paying More." *The New York Times.* February 20:1, 24.

Johnston. D. K. 2003. *Perfectly Legal: The Covert Campaign to Rig Our Tax System to Benefit the Super Rich—and Cheat Everybody Else.* New York: Penguin.

Kanter, R. M. 1977. *Men and Women of the Corporation.* New York: Basic Books.

Kaufman, D. R. 1989. "Professional Women: How Real Are the Recent Gains?" In *Women, a Feminist Perspective,* 329–346, edited by Jo Freeman. Palo Alto: Mayfield Publishing Company.

Kirkpatrick, David. 2006. "G.O.P. Moderates Rebuff Lobbyists, Then Woo Them." *The New York Times.* April 30:A26.

Kuersten, A. K. and J. Jagemann. 2000. "Does the Interest Group Choir Really 'Sing with an Upper Class Accent?' Coalitions of Race and Gender Groups Before the Supreme Court." *Women & Politics.* 21(3):53–73.

Lieberman, T. 1999. "Social Security for Women." *The Nation.* 269:6.

Lorber, J. 1989. "Trust, Loyalty, and the Place of Women in the Informal Organization of Work." In *Women, a Feminist Perspective,* 347–355, edited by Jo Freeman. Palo Alto: Mayfield Publishing Company.

Manke, B., Seery, B. L., Crouter, A.C., McHale, S. M. 1994. "The Three Corners of Domestic Labor: Mothers,' Fathers,' and Children's Weekday and Weekend Housework." *Journal of Marriage and the Family.* 56:657–668.

Marable. M. 1995. "Black Intellectuals in Conflict." *New Politics.* 5:35–40.

Marceau, J. 1989. *A Family Business? The Making of an International Business Elite.* Cambridge: Cambridge University Press.

Martin, P.Y. 1993. "Multiple Gender Contexts and Employee Rewards." *Work and Occupations.* 20:296–336.

Martin, P. Y. 1996. "Gendering and Evaluating Dynamics: Men, Masculinities, and Managements." In *Men as Managers, Men as Men,* 186–209, edited by D. Collinson and J. Hearn. London: Sage.

Martin, P. Y. 2001. "Mobilizing Masculinities': Women's Experiences of Men at Work." *Organization.* 8(4): 587–618.

Martin, P.Y. 2003. "'Said and Done' Versus 'Saying and Doing'" *Gender & Society.* 17(3):342–366.

Martin, P.Y. and D. L. Collinson. 1999. "Gender and Sexuality in Organizations." In *Revisioning Gender,* 285–310, edited by Myra Marx Ferree, Judith Lorber, and Beth B. Hess. London: Sage.

McCafferty, E. J. 1997. *Taxing Women.* Chicago: University of Chicago Press.

Mintz, B. 2002. "Elites and Politics: The Corporate Elite and the Capitalist Class in the United States. *Research in Political Sociology.* 11:53–77.

Mintz, B. and M. Schwartz. 1985. *The Power Structure of American Business.* Chicago: University of Chicago Press.

Misra, J. 1998a. "The Welfare State and Women: Structure, Agency, and Diversity." *Social Politics.* 5:259–285.

Misra, J. 1998b. "Mothers and Workers? The Value of Women's Labor: Women and the Emergence of Family Allowance Policy." *Gender & Society.* 12:376–399.

Misra, J. 2002. "Class, Race, and Gender and Theorizing Welfare States." *Research in Political Sociology.* 11:19–52.

Mitchell, Alison. 2001. "Congressional Republicans See Bush's Big Tax Cut, and Think Bigger." *The New York Times.* February 7:13.

Moore, G. 1987. "Women in the Old-Boy Network: The Case of New York Government." In *Power Elites and Organizations,* 63–84, edited by G. William Domhoff and Thomas Dye. Beverly Hills: Sage. Moore, G. 1988. "Women in Elite Positions: Insiders or Outsiders?" *Sociological Forum.* 3:566–585.

Moore, G. 1990. "Structural Determinants of Men's and Women's Personal Networks." *American Sociological Review* 55:726–735.

Morgen, S. and A. Bookman. 1988. "Rethinking Women and Politics: An Introductory Essay." In *Women and the Politics of Empowerment,* 3–32, edited by Ann Bookman and Sandra Morgan. Philadelphia: Temple University Press.

National Center for Policy Analysis (NCPA). 2002. "Social Security Penalizes Women Who Work, Pay Taxes; Dual-Earner Taxes Far Exceed Extra Benefits." April 9:1008099.

National Council of Women's Organizations [NCWO]. 2005 "The Augusta National Golf Club Story." www.womensorganizations.org.

Neustadtl, A., D. Scott, D. Clawson. 1991. "Class Struggle In Campaign Finance? Political Action Committee Contributions in the 1984 Elections." *Sociological Forum.* 6:219–238.

Nickel, H. 2000. "Winning Her Place At the Rail." *Illinois Issues.* March:1–3, www.lib.niu.edu/ipo.

Nownes, A. and P. Freeman. 1998. "Female Lobbyists: Women in the World of the "Good Ol' Boys." *The Journal of Politics.* 60:1181–1201.

Olsson, K. 2002. "Ghostwriting the Law." *Mother Jones.* September/October, www.motherjones.com/news/outfront/2002/09.

Orloff, A. 1996. "Gender in the Welfare State." *Annual Review of Sociology.* 22:51–78.

Orloff, A. 2001. "Ending the Entitlements of Poor Single Mothers: Changing Social Policies, Women's Employment, and Caregiving in the Contemporary United States." In *Women and Welfare: Theory and Practice in the United States and Europe,* 133–159, edited by Nancy Hirschmann and Ulrike Leibert. New Brunswick: Rutgers University Press.

References

2222153

2

Parsons, T. and R. F. Bales. 1955. *Family, Socialization and Interaction Process.* Glencoe, IL: The Free Press.

Perrucci, R. and E. Wysong. 2002. "The Global Economy and the Privileged Class," In *Working in America: Continuity, Conflict, and Change,* 173–187, edited by S. Wharton. Second Edition. New York: McGraw Hill.

Pitkin, H. 1972. *Wittgenstein and Justice.* Berkeley: University of California Press.

Pleck, J. H. 1985. *Working Husbands/Working Wives.* Beverly Hills: Sage Publications

Postrel, V. 2000. "The U.S. Tax System is Discouraging Married Women From Working." *The New York Times.* November 2:C2.

Postrel, V. 2003. "Wives' Tale: The 'Marriage Penalty' Taxes Women for Working, Not Wedding." *Boston Globe.* April 13:E1.

Prechel, H. 2000. *Big Business and the State: Historical Transitions and Corporate Transformation, 1980–1990s.* Albany,: State University of New York Press.

Prechel, H. 2003. "Historical Contingency Theory, Policy Paradigm Shifts, and Corporate Malfeasance at the Turn of the 21st Century." *Research in Political Sociology.* 12:311–340.

Public Affairs Council. 2005. "New Report, State of Corporate Public Affairs Packed With Findings on Fast-Changing Profession; Number of Corporate D.C. Offices Up." P.R. Newswire Association, LLC. October 20:1

Reskin, B. and P. Phipps. 1988. "Women in Male-Dominated Professional and Managerial Occupations." In *Women Working,* 190–205, edited by A. Stromberg and S. Harkness. Mountain View, CA: Mayfield.

Reskin, B. and I. Padavic. 2002. *Women and Men at Work.* New York: Sage Publications.

Roche, Walter. 2005. "The Nation: Nominee is Linked to Controversy." *The Los Angeles Times.* July 29:A10.

Rothstein, B. 2005. "Women with Weapons Bonding In the Woods." *The Hill.* 21.

Ryan, M. 1979. "The Power of Women's Networks: A Case Study of Female Moral

Reform in Antebellum America. *Feminist Studies.* 5(1):66–70.

Sabato, L. 1984. *PAC Power: Inside the World of Political Action Committees.* New York: Norton.

Sacks, K. 1988. "Gender and Grass Roots Leadership." In *Women and the Politics of Empowerment,* 77–96, edited by A. Bookman and S. Morgen. Philadelphia: Temple University Press.

St. Louis Post-Dispatch. 2005. "Educators on K St. Art to Come." Editorial. 49.

Saltzman Chafetz, J. 1997. "I Need a (Traditional) Wife! Employment-Family Conflicts." In *Workplace/Women's Place,* 116–124, edited by Dana Dunn. Los Angeles: Roxbury Publishing.

Schlozman, K. L. and J. T. Tierney. 1986. *Organized Interests and American Democracy.* New York: Harper & Row.

Schmidt, Susan. 2004. "Indian Tribe Paid to Influence Bill, Files Show." *Houston Chronicle.* November 16:16.

Schmidt, Susan and James Grimaldi. 2005. "How a Lobbyist Stacked the Deck." *The Washington Post.* October 16:A01.

Schwartz, M. (ed.). 1987. *The Structure of Power in America: The Corporate Elite as a Ruling Class.* New York: Holmes & Meier.

Scott, D. 1991. "Beyond PAC-Man: The Significance of Gender Difference in Corporate-Government Relations." *Sociological Practice Review.* 2:252–263.

Scott, D. 1996. "Shattering the Instrumental-Expressive Myth: The Power of Women's Networks in Corporate-Government Affairs." *Gender & Society.* 10:232–247.

Scott, J. 1999. "Some Reflections on Gender and Politics." In *Revisioning Gender,* 70–96, edited by Myra Marx Ferree, Judith Lorber, and Beth B. Hess. Thousand Oaks, CA: Sage.

Shelton, B. A. and D. John. 1993. "Does Marital Status Make a Difference? Housework Among Married and Cohabiting Men and Women." *Journal of Family Issues.* 14:401–423.

Shennon, Phillip. 2006. "Lobbying Cases Highlight Prime Targets' Family Ties." *The New York Times.* April 9:A26.

Simon, R. J. and G. Danziger. 1991. *Women's Movements in America.* New York: Praeger.

Smith, D. 1984. "The Deep Structure of Gender Antitheses: Another View of Capitalism and Patriarchy." *Humanity and Society.* 8:395–406.

Smith, Jeffrey R. 2005. "DeLay's Travel Expenses lead to Nonprofit, Lobbyist." *Houston Chronicle.* April 24:4.

Smith, Jeffrey R. 2006. "E-Mails show Effort to Fudge Cost of DeLay's Trip." *The Washington Post.* May 7:A9.

Smith-Lovin, L. and J. M. McPherson. 1993. "You Are Who You Know: A Network Approach to Gender." In *Theory on Gender, Feminism on Theory,* 223–251, edited by P. England. New York: Aldine.

South, S. and G. Spitze 1994. "Housework in Marital and Nonmarital Households." *American Sociological Review.* 59:327–347.

Stolberg, Sheryl Gay. 2006a. "Senate Approves Lobbying Limits By Wide Margin." *The New York Times.* March 30:A1.

Stolberg, Sheryl Gay. 2006b. "Push to Tighten Lobbying Rules Loses Strength." *The New York Times.* March 11:A1.

Stone, P. 1999. "Gimme Shelter." *National Journal.* April 10:944–947.

Thorne, B. 1993. *Gender Play.* New Brunswick, NJ: Rutgers University Press.

U.S. Bureau of the Census. 2000, Statistical Abstracts.

U.S. Bureau of the Census. 2004. "Current Population Survey."

U.S. Bureau of the Census. 2005. "CPS Annual Social and Economic Supplement."

U.S. Department of Labor Statistics. 2005. "Women in the Labor Force: A Databook." May.

Vanek, J. 1983. "Household Work, Wage Work, and Sexual Equality." In *Family in Transition,* fourth edition, edited by Alene Skolnick and Jerome H. Skolnick. Glenview, IL: Scott, Foresman and Company.

Vieth, W. 2005. "A Woman Takes on Social Security Overhaul: Former Business Lobbyist Leanne Abdnor Is Among Those Championing Bush's Personal Retirement Account Plan." *Los Angeles Times.* March 30:A15.

Wagman, B. and Nancy F. 1988. "The Feminization of Inequality: Some News Patterns. *Challenge: The Magazine of Economic Affairs.* November/December.

Warner, J. 2005. *Perfect Madness: Motherhood in the Age of Anxiety.* New York: Riverhead Books.

Washington Representatives. 1980, 1986, and 1995 Annual Editions. Washington, D.C.: Columbia Books.

Wellman, B., P. Carrington, A. Hall. 1988. Networks as Personal Communities." In *Social Structures: A Network Approach,* 130–184, edited by B. Wellman and S. D. Berkowitz. Cambridge, England: Cambridge University Press.

Wetzstein, C. 1996. "Group Aims to Rally Women Behind Tax Cuts." *The Washington Times.* August 22:4.

Wharton, C. S. 1994. "Finding Time for the 'Second Shift': The Impact of Flexible Work Schedules on Women's Double Days." *Gender & Society.* 3:189–205.

Whitaker, Katie. 2002. *Mad Madge.* New York:Basic Books.

Williamson, J. B. and S. Rix. 2000. "Social Security Reform: Implications for Women." *Journal of Aging and Social Policy.* 11(4):41–68.

Yogev, Sara. 1984. "Do Professional Women Really Have Egalitarian Marital Relationships?" *Journal of Marriage and Family.* 43:865–871.

Zweigenhaft, R. 1987. "Minorities and Women of the Corporation: Will They Attain Seats of Power?" In *Power Elites and Organizations,* 37–62, edited by G. W. Domhoff and T. Dye. Beverly Hills, CA: Sage.

Zweigenhaft, R. and G. W. Domhoff. 1998. *Diversity in the Power Elite: Have Women and Minorities Reached the Top?* New Haven, CT: Yale University Press.

Zweigenhaft, Richard. 2001. "Diversity in the United States Power Elite." *Journal of International Migration and Integration.* Volume 2, Number 2.

Index

Abdnor, Leanne, 47
abortion, 7, 23, 24
Abramoff, Jack: high-powered
lobbyist, 136; Norquist's, 145n3;
scandal, 4–6, 27, 29
Abramoff, Pamela, 6
access, through networking,
84–90
Ackelsberg, Martha, 66
African American: community,
73; middle-class, 72; old age
and poverty, 62; poor women,
61–62; positions in organizations, 73; problems, 72–73; professionals, 72; racial and ethnic
consciousness and unity, 75;
underrepresented in prestigious
law schools, 128; women, 22;
women working outside the
home, 58
age: and poverty, in women of
color, 62; and women, 70
Alliance for Worker Retirement
Security, 48
American Express, 48
American Female Moral Reform
Society, 20
Americans for Tax Reform, 4, 36
American League of Lobbyists,
29

Americans for Tax Reform,
145n3
Ameritech, 39
animal rights, 24
Anthony, Susan B., 23
anti-gambling legislation, 4
Anti-Slavery Convention of
American Women, 20
Appelbaum, Richard P., 142
AT&T, 23
Augusta National Golf Club, 36,
128–129

Bandow, Doug, 5
Bangladesh, 141
Bartlett, L. D., 3
Bath, M. G., 38
Bendix, 26–27
benefits of family ties, 102–125
Bermuda tax-avoidance scheme,
53
Bill of Rights, 73
birthing, 107, 109
Bohemian Grove: analysis of,
76–77, 98; Lakeside Talks, 85;
old-boys network, 6, 135; ritual
activities, 82
Bohemian Grove (Domhoff), 83
Bonacich, Edna, 142
Bookman, A., 8, 44

breakfast club, 110–112
Brewster, Bill, 40
Brewster, Suzie, 36
Buckman, Edwin, 6
Buckman, Wendy, 6
Burk, Martha, 36, 128–129
Burning Tree golf course, 128
Bush, George: choice for secretary of the Treasury, 69; corporate scandals, 5; funding studies, commissioning of, 47; private social security accounts, 57; tax cuts, 51, 52–55
business: -government partnership, 77, 79–84, 98, 136–137, 139; Tax Alliance retreat and, 76–77
Business Council, 135
business hegemony, 64–70

capitalist economy, 141
career advancement, 138
caretakers, women as, 64, 107–108
"caring tax," 59
Carter, Jimmy, 25
Cato, 47
"cattle calls," 110. *See also* fundraisers
Cavendish, Margaret (duchess of Windsor), 19
Center for Public Integrity, 28
Center for Responsive Politics, 13
Cheney, Dick, 5
children: care of, 105–106, 111, 116, 122–123; issues of, 18; networking opportunities and, 119
China, 141
Christian Coalition, 4

Christian Science Monitor, 54
Citizens for Tax Justice, 13
class: bias, in tax and social security policy, 62–64; dynamics of, 142
Clawson, D., 9
Clinton, Bill, 69
clubs. *See* social club memberships
Colgan, Celeste, 63
Colgate-Palmolive, 52
Collins, S., 73
compensation, 42–43
conflict of interest, 71–75
Congressional Country Club, 118
connections, making, 30–38, 114–125. *See also* networking activities; networks; work networks
Conway, Bess, 36
Copley News Service, 5
corporate advancement for women, 26–27, 98
corporate government affairs: growth of operations, 25–26; hierarchy of, 26; titles in, 26–27
corporate hegemony, 140
corporate lobbying: bottom line, 41–46; from "private" to "public," 19–24; growth of government relations operations, 25–26; number of offices in Washington, 25, 126; surge in women in, 24–27, 102; women and power, 126–142; women's entrance into, 18–19, 26. *See also* lobbying
Corporate Patriot Enforcement Act, 5

"family wage," 143n2

family work, 105–106; gender differences in, 102, 107–109, 115; limiting women's success, 104; unequal division of, 103; unrecognized type of work, 134–135

FBI. *See* Federal Bureau of Investigation

Federal Bureau of Investigation (FBI), 6, 55

femininity: doing, 134; hegemonic, 99–100; women and, 140

feminized activities, 133, 145n1

Flanigan, Timothy, 5

Folbre, Nancy, 53, 56, 59, 60, 72

Ford Motor Company, 68

foreign: -based corporations, 54; competition, 141

Francis, David, 54

Freeman, P., 18, 38, 40

friendships: in the workplace, 104; made at Tax Alliance retreat, 87–89 , 95–96

fundraisers, 31–35, 110

Gap, 141

Gayvert-Owen, J., 38

GDP. *See* gross domestic product (GDP), 51–52

gender: bias in tax and social security policy, 62–64; differences, 38–41, 102, 107–109; do—, 76–101, 136, 143n1; dynamics of, 142; equality, 74–75; family relations and, 105; ideologies, 58, 141; inequalities, 42–46, 74–75, 106, 110–111, 132–133; neutrality and public policy, 132; public policy and,

141; significance of, 90–98; stratification, 8; Tax Alliance retreat and—interests, 76–77, 98–101

General Motors, 50, 52

Georgetown University, 100

Gerstel, N., 103

Ghiloni, B. W., 42

gift tax, 50

"girls" networks. *See* network activities; networks

global economy, 141, 142

GNP. *See* gross national product

golfing, 35–38

government-business partnership, 77, 79–84, 98, 136–137, 139

government relations managers profile, 105–106

Gramsci, Antonio, 68

gross domestic product (GDP), 51–52

Gross, H. E., 103

gross national product (GNP), 59

"guerilla" groups, 135, 145n2

gun control, 24

Hanchard, M., 72

Hartmann, H., 58

Hartsock, N., 8

Harvard University, 100

head-of-households, 61, 70

health care: funding deprivation, 56–57; issues, 24, 85, 100; lobbying, 7

Heberle, R., 48

hegemonic: femininity, 99–100; masculinity, 131–135, 140

hegemony: business, 64–70; Gramsci's definition of, 68

ABOUT THE AUTHOR

DENISE BENOIT received her Ph.D. from the University of Massachusetts at Amherst and is an associate professor of sociology at the State University of New York, Geneseo. She has written extensively on the topic of gender and corporate–government relations. She is coauthor of *Money Talks: Corporate PACs and Political Influence*.